Key Terms
in Philosophy
of Art

BLOOMSBURY *KEY TERMS*

The *Key Terms* series offers undergraduate students clear, concise and accessible introductions to core topics. Each book includes a comprehensive overview of the key terms, concepts, thinkers and texts in the area covered and ends with a guide to further resources.

Available now:

Key Terms in Ethics, Oskari Kuusela
Key Terms in Logic, edited by Jon Williamson and Federica Russo
Key Terms in Philosophy of Mind, Pete Mandik
Key Terms in Philosophy of Religion, Raymond VanArragon

KEY TERMS

Key Terms in Philosophy of Art

TIGER C. ROHOLT

BLOOMSBURY
LONDON · NEW DELHI · NEW YORK · SYDNEY

Bloomsbury Academic

An imprint of Bloomsbury Publishing Plc

50 Bedford Square
London
WC1B 3DP
UK

1385 Broadway
New York
NY 10018
USA

www.bloomsbury.com

Bloomsbury is a registered trade mark of Bloomsbury Publishing Plc

First published 2013

©Tiger C. Roholt, 2013

British Library Cataloguing-in-Publication Data

A catalogue record for this book is available from the British Library.

ISBN: HB: 978-0-8264-2162-3
PB: 978-0-8264-3527-9
ePDF: 978-1-4411-5891-8
ePub: 978-1-4411-3246-8

Library of Congress Cataloging-in-Publication Data

A catalogue record for this book is available from the Library of Congress.

Typeset by Deanta Global Publishing Services, Chennai, India
Printed and bound in India

For Shira

CONTENTS

ACKNOWLEDGMENTS

I am appreciative of those who reviewed this book's proposal, as well as the editors at Bloomsbury/Continuum who have been encouraging, helpful, and patient: Colleen Coalter and Sarah Campbell.

Over the years I have enjoyed the kindness and support of numerous individuals in the philosophy of art community—too many to mention here; however, I would like to acknowledge Hanne Appelqvist, Christopher Bartel, Sherrill Begres, David Clowney, Marcia Eaton, Lydia Goehr, Theodore Gracyk, Keith Gunderson, Michael Kelly, Jerrold Levinson, Margaret Moore, Jonathan Neufeld, Henry Pratt, and Brian Soucek.

I would like to sincerely thank my departmental colleagues at Montclair State University for welcoming me so warmly—David Benfield (a true mentor), Mark Clatterbuck, Cynthia Eller, Roland Garrett, Christopher Herrera, Yasir Ibrahim, Stephen Johnson, Michael Kogan, Kirk McDermid, Dorothy Rogers, and Lise Vail. I thank the many students in my philosophy of art courses who have matched my enthusiasm for the subject, and have taken our discussions so seriously; I enjoy these discussions and have learned a lot from them.

This book is dedicated to my good-hearted, creative, and intelligent daughter, Shira Gal Roholt (almost nine years old as I write this). Her grandparents, Dorothy and Les Roholt, have always been unconditionally supportive of my various endeavors; they seem to have taken me seriously from the time I was three years old. Going back one generation, I had the good fortune to know Ruby and Bill Smith, my maternal grandparents, who had an enormous influence upon me. I am also very appreciative of the kindness of the Rosenberg family.

Finally, I want to express my heartfelt gratitude to Jill Rosenberg for spirited and challenging discussions about writing, art, philosophy, and everything else, but more importantly for helping me—us—to flourish in the face of life's challenges.

PREFACE

This book is written for students who are approaching the philosophy of art for the first time. I have attempted to use straightforward language to provide basic, clear descriptions and explanations of the subject matter. I conceive of the book as a platform that will help students to understand the material in their courses. The book is shaped by a specific notion of what it means to be effectively introduced to the philosophy of art. Unlike the philosophy of mind (say), and more like ethics, a student encountering the philosophy of art for the first time should encounter the philosophical tradition, the foundations. Understanding what Plato, Kant, and Hegel have to say about art is often required for understanding contemporary philosophers. Perhaps more importantly, familiarity with the tradition presents a student with a broad and deep view of the philosophy of art's scope and potential (which is different from the view of the subfield one might obtain from a survey of the work of philosophers at a particular period in its history). These beliefs have guided my selection of entries as well as the content of the entries. That said, the student will find ample consideration of contemporary issues, including entries on contemporary American philosophers, such as Arthur Danto and Kendall Walton, as well as entries on influential twentieth-century European figures, such as Martin Heidegger and Theodor W. Adorno.

How to read this book

The book consists of four main chapters—Key Terms, Key Thinkers, Key Texts, and The Arts. The entries in each chapter are organized alphabetically. The Key Terms chapter, the largest, consists of introductory overviews of the main concepts, issues, and approaches in the philosophy of art. The contents of the Key Thinkers chapter is self-explanatory but notice that the Key Texts section contains a more thorough consideration of texts written by some of the key thinkers (in these cases, within a given thinker's entry, I direct the reader to the relevant entry in the Key Texts chapter). For readers interested in finding their way into the philosophy of art by focusing upon one particular art form, The Arts chapter includes entries on architecture, dance, film, literature, music, photography, tragedy, and visual art. These entries highlight thought-provoking philosophical issues that emerge in relation to each art form, and in addition, you will find many references in these entries to the book's other entries.

You may want to use this book simply for looking up various terms, thinkers, texts, and art forms as you encounter them in your studies. But this book is also written so that you can read it straight through. However you approach it, *I strongly recommend* beginning with the introduction and sections in the Key Terms chapter that anchor the book—VALUE OF ART and DEFINING ART. The numerous, internal cross-references are a powerful feature of this book; think of these as hyperlinks. When you see a word in SMALL CAPS—finish the entry you are reading first, then—turn to the "linked" entry in order to obtain more information and/or more context regarding that term, text or thinker; this will enable you to develop a deeper, broader understanding of the set of issues at hand. Occasionally, you will find a different form of a term employed (e.g., "ONTOLOGICAL") to refer to an entry ("ONTOLOGY"). Even though this is a small book, by following the hyperlinks, you can delve quite deeply into specific issues and thinkers.

This book includes a useful index; if you are looking for information about a particular philosopher, for example, but find that there is no devoted entry, check the index; there may be a discussion of the philosopher in a term entry. For example, although there is no entry devoted to Maurice Merleau-Ponty or Roman Ingarden, you will find some discussion of their work in the PHENOMENOLOGY entry. In the index, if a term, name, or text has a devoted entry, the page number of that entry is given in bold. The index will also include authors' names not considered in an entry but included in an entry's "further reading" list.

Since the entries in this book are intended to give the reader only an introductory overview of the issues, ultimately, a student will want to fill out her understanding through coursework or further individual study. For this purpose, I have included very specific suggestions for further reading after each section, as well as a section at the end of the book—A Guide to Further Reading—which lists many *general* texts for further reading. There are a few different categories of resources a student might look to in addition to this book. First, obviously, there are primary texts; in addition to the key texts discussed in this book, a number of additional primary texts are suggested following various entries. Second, there are anthologies of primary readings, such as *Reading Aesthetics and Philosophy of Art: Selected Texts with Interactive Commentary*, edited by Christopher Janaway (Wiley-Blackwell, 2005); a number of additional anthologies are listed in A Guide to Further Reading. The section also includes a list of general companions and handbooks, such as *The Oxford Handbook of Aesthetics*, edited by Jerrold Levinson (Oxford University Press, 2005); such books typically consist of chapters devoted to issues and concepts at the core of the field. Introductory texts constitute another category, for example, Stephen Davies's *The Philosophy of Art* (Wiley-Blackwell, 2006). A number of additional introductions are also listed in the section on Further Reading. Finally, the student will want to know about the extremely useful, four-volume *Encyclopedia of Aesthetics*, edited by Michael Kelly (Oxford University Press, 1998).

INTRODUCTION

What is the philosophy of art?

Why do we care about art? What is art? Is there some quality common to all works of art? What kind of a *thing* is a work of art? (Is a work of art a physical object? A mental entity? An abstract object?) On what grounds do we judge or evaluate works of art? Are such AESTHETIC JUDGMENTS subjective or objective? What is AESTHETIC EXPERIENCE? What is the relationship between art and ETHICS? What is the relationship between art and POLITICS? What is the relationship between art and the EMOTIONS?

The philosophy of art addresses these and many other questions. Here is one way to think about what philosophers of art do: they explore issues that artists, critics, art historians, and art enthusiasts tend to take for granted or neglect. A philosophy of art (i.e., a philosophical theory of art, as opposed to a sociological or psychological theory of art) aims to offer an answer to some core cluster of the questions above. At a minimum, a philosophical theory of art aims to help us to determine which things are works of art and aims to explain why we value art; the most informative theories will also endeavor to provide some guidance for evaluating individual works of art.

These issues of DEFINING ART and the VALUE OF ART are central. Regarding definition, philosophers have attempted to define art by focusing upon a particular feature of works of art, a function, or contextual relation. It has been suggested, for example, that art can be defined in terms of REPRESENTATION, "significant form" (see FORMALISM; Clive BELL), the affordance of AESTHETIC EXPERIENCE (see John DEWEY; Monroe BEARDSLEY), the EXPRESSION of EMOTION (see R. G. COLLINGWOOD), and so on. Some philosophers locate the value of art in the above defining characteristics; for example, art may be valuable because it performs the function of expressing emotions. A number of other conceptions of art's value have been suggested. Perhaps, most simply, art is valuable because perceiving it is pleasant. More deeply, perhaps art is valuable in that the best works of art can convey the values of a culture (see G. W. F. HEGEL). Perhaps art is valuable in that the best works of music (say) foster in listeners independent thinking and a critical disposition (see Theodor W. ADORNO).

What do philosophers of art mean by "Art?"

Art's ubiquity in different periods and cultures suggests that the basic impetus to sing, dance, draw, and make up stories has evolutionary origins. Although PLATO and ARISTOTLE wrote about poetry, painting, music, and so on, they conceived of the arts differently than we do (see DEFINING ART). In our culture, in the modern West, we employ a specific notion of art. Since the eighteenth century, it has been common to categorize painting, sculpture, music, poetry, and architecture as "the fine arts," *les beaux arts* (some thinkers, such as Charles Batteux, disputed architecture's inclusion). At that time, these arts were grouped together based on conceptions of BEAUTY, the AESTHETIC, pleasure, and imitation (see REPRESENTATION). Since the eighteenth century, this list of art forms has grown; we now typically take prose literature, film, photography, dance, and so on, to be classified as fine arts. The concept, *art*, examined by philosophers of art today is, by and large, this one.

Philosophy: Analytic and Continental

The reader may be surprised to learn that many of the great philosophers of the tradition have written at length about art—Plato, Aristotle, David Hume, Immanuel Kant, G. W. F. Hegel, Friedrich Nietzsche, Martin Heidegger, John Dewey, and others (see the entries on all of these philosophers, in the "Key Thinkers" and "Key Texts" sections). While the work of these philosophers is very diverse, they all employ arguments. There are, of course, different kinds of arguments, but in the most basic sense, philosophers put forward claims, and support these claims with reasons. This general activity drives analytic as well as continental philosophy. Analytic philosophy is the dominant Anglo-American tradition; analytic philosophers put a premium on clarity and argumentative rigor; some analytic philosophers have claimed that the main business of analytic philosophy is to analyze concepts. As Noël Carroll writes in his *Philosophy of Art*, "The purpose of the analytic philosophy of art is to explore the concepts that make creating and thinking about art possible. Some of these concepts include: the very concept of art itself, as well as the concepts of representation, expression, artistic form, and aesthetics" (1999, p. 5). (See DEFINING ART for an example.)

What, then, is continental philosophy? Since the second half of the twentieth century, Anglo-American philosophers have drawn a distinction between analytic and continental philosophy. Analytic and continental philosophers share the philosophical tradition, from ancient Greek philosophy through Immanuel KANT (1724–1804); following Kant, the traditions diverge. The subsequent, specifically continental tradition involves a handful of often disparate movements, built upon differing methodologies and assumptions— nineteenth-century German philosophy (see HEGEL, SCHOPENHAUER); phenomenology and existentialism (see PHENOMENOLOGY, NIETZSCHE, HEIDEGGER); Marxism and critical theory (see MARXISM, ADORNO, BENJAMIN); structuralism, poststructuralism, and postmodernism (see BARTHES, BOURDIEU, LITERATURE). One way to conceive of the continental tradition is that these philosophers resist examining the issues they investigate in the abstract; they typically consider their subject matter within a sociopolitical context (Marxism and critical theory), a historical context (Hegel and German idealism), or a context of lived-experience (phenomenology)—or some combination of these contexts. (Especially in recent decades, some analytic philosophers have begun to consider such contexts as well.) This book, while designed to emphasize the analytic philosophy of art, and written primarily in the analytic style, includes more continental philosophy of art than may be expected in a reference book of this kind and size. Continental views are not only included in the *thinker, text*, and *arts* entries; they are also integrated into the *term* entries, where appropriate.

One last introductory issue: the philosophy of art is occasionally referred to as AESTHETICS; this is problematic. Properly speaking, aesthetics has to do with the issues surrounding the aesthetic experience of art and NATURE, including BEAUTY and other AESTHETIC PROPERTIES. Philosophers of art address many issues that simply do not involve aesthetics, properly understood. In recent decades, even general philosophical theories of art have been put forward that do not center on aesthetics; in fact, some theories do not involve aesthetics at all (e.g., Arthur DANTO).

Further Reading for this entry

Carroll, N. (1999), *Philosophy of Art: A Contemporary Introduction.* London: Routledge Press.
Cooper, D. E. (1994), "The presidential address: Analytical and continental philosophy." *Proceedings of the Aristotelian Society*, 94: 1–18.
Kristeller, P. O. (1951), "The modern system of the arts: A study in the history of aesthetics." *Journal of the History of Ideas*, 12: 496–527 and 13: 17–46.

DETAILED LIST

OF SECTIONS

Key Terms

Key Thinkers

Adorno, Theodor W.
Aristotle
Barthes, Roland
Beardsley, Monroe
Bell, Clive
Benjamin, Walter
Bourdieu, Pierre
Collingwood, Robin George
Danto, Arthur Coleman
Dewey, John
Goodman, Nelson
Hegel, Georg Wilhelm Friedrich
Heidegger, Martin
Hume, David
Kant, Immanuel
Nietzsche, Friedrich
Plato
Schopenhauer, Arthur
Sibley, Frank Noel
Walton, Kendall
Wollheim, Richard

Key Texts

Aristotle, *Poetics*
Bell, Clive, *Art*
Collingwood, R. G., *Principles of Art*
Dewey, John, *Art as Experience*
Hegel, G. W. F., *Lectures on Fine Art*
Heidegger, Martin, "The Origin of the Work of Art"
Hume, David, "Of the Standard of Taste"
Kant, Immanuel, *Critique of Judgment*
Plato, *The Republic*

The Arts

Key Terms

Aesthetic

The term "aesthetics" is often used loosely to refer to the philosophy of art, but it has a more precise meaning, with origins in the ancient Greek word "*aisthēsis*." The Greek word denotes ordinary sense perception; "the aesthetic," as introduced into philosophy in the eighteenth century by Alexander Baumgarten (1714–62), referred to *pleasing perceptions of* BEAUTY. The eighteenth century was a crucial period for the modern philosophy of art, as this was the period during which the category of the fine arts solidified (see the introduction). "Aesthetic" has a similar sense in common usage even today. When a person points to something, designer stationery (say), and remarks that it is "aesthetic," he probably means that it is beautiful, pleasing to the eye. However, as beauty has come to occupy a less central role in the arts, the meaning of "aesthetic" in the philosophy of art has changed; it has been common, for some time, to refer to objects or experiences as aesthetic even in cases where it would seem forced or simply incorrect to call them beautiful; for example, one may take a certain demolished building or a punk rock guitar riff to be aesthetic while not considering them to be beautiful. This eliminates a key element of the definition, but philosophers still understand the aesthetic to be perception-centered, pleasing, and valuable (see VALUE OF ART).

Philosophers often seek a more precise understanding of the term by examining related concepts—the aesthetic attitude (see DISINTEREST), AESTHETIC EXPERIENCE, AESTHETIC JUDGMENT, AESTHETIC PROPERTY, aesthetic value, aesthetic pleasure, aesthetic object (see PHENOMENOLOGY), and so on. The thought is that properties, experiences, and so on, which are aesthetic, are special in some way; the hope is that if we can clarify exactly what (say) an aesthetic property is, then we will be able to define aesthetic experience in terms of these properties, and this will help us to clarify the other concepts, as well as the aesthetic itself. Different philosophers have taken different concepts to be primary—some, for instance, claim that a thing is aesthetic primarily because of the experience it affords (see DEWEY; BEARDSLEY) or the properties it possesses (see SIBLEY). Other philosophers believe that the nature and value of art are not elucidated through an examination of the aesthetic (see DEFINING ART, ADORNO, DANTO, DICKIE, HEIDEGGER).

Further Reading

Baumgarten, A. G. (1961 [1750–58]), *Aesthetica*. Hildesheim: George Holms Verlagsbuchhandlung.

Beardsley, M. (1966), *Aesthetics from Classical Greece to the Present*. New York: Macmillan.

Eaton, M. M. (2004), "Art and the Aesthetic," in P. Kivy (ed.), *The Blackwell Guide to Aesthetics*. Oxford: Wiley-Blackwell.

Goldman, A. (2005), "The Aesthetic," in D. M. Lopes and B. Gaut (eds), *The Routledge Companion to Aesthetics*. New York: Routledge Press.

Aesthetic Attitude, see Disinterest

Aesthetic Experience

An AESTHETIC experience is a particular state of mind that philosophers attempt to distinguish from other states of mind. At the very least, an aesthetic experience is an experience that is valued for its own sake. John DEWEY takes aesthetic experiences to be unified by an intense, pervasive quality that has been developed and accentuated; aesthetic experiences are complete in the sense that they reach a kind of consummation. In his early work, Monroe BEARDSLEY's account of aesthetic experience resembled Dewey's: an aesthetic experience is complex, intense, and unified. Later, Beardsley acknowledges that many experiences have an aesthetic character but lack the unity required to classify them as aesthetic experiences. His account of the broader notion of *the aesthetic in experience* (i.e., experience with an aesthetic character) is set out in terms of five criteria. He takes the first criterion, object directedness, to be necessary. Any three of the final four criteria are necessary: felt freedom, detached affect, active discovery, and wholeness. Beardsley's earlier view focused on properties of the experience itself, whereas his later view focuses on the object of experience; recent accounts of aesthetic experience have followed the latter approach.

A number of philosophers, including Dewey, emphasize that aesthetic experience is active, not passive. R. G. COLLINGWOOD, for example, maintains that a spectator has imaginative work to do in order to perceive an artwork correctly. Roman Ingarden holds that the unfinished aspects of works of art must be "concretized" by spectators (see PHENOMENOLOGY).

One kind of definition of art is a functional definition; one kind of functional definition is based on aesthetic experience: an artifact that affords an aesthetic experience is a work of art (see DEFINING ART, BEARDSLEY). Consider two commonly cited reasons that such a definition fails. First, we occasionally have aesthetic experiences of objects that are clearly not works of art, such as a waterfall, a designer stickynote, or a scientific theory. Another problem with aesthetic definitions is that many works of art seem not to have to do with aesthetic experience at all, such as CONCEPTUAL ART and ready-mades (see DANTO, DICKIE).

Many accounts of aesthetic experience involve a certain *detached* perceptual approach to experiencing works of art (interestingly, John DEWEY's does not). Philosophers have referred to this detachment with different terms (and there are differences in the details of how this detachment is specified); it is, perhaps, most commonly referred to as DISINTEREST, but one also finds "psychical distance," the "aesthetic attitude," and so on. The main idea is that in order to perceive works of art correctly, they must be approached with this sort of detached perceptual comportment. Immanuel KANT developed a notion of disinterest in the context of his account of AESTHETIC JUDGMENT. For Arthur SCHOPENHAUER, disinterest has relevance even beyond art. FORMALISTS typically invoke some notion of disinterest in order to make sense of a perceiver's focusing only on a work of art's design. Edward Bullough's "psychical distance" involves putting "out of gear" the practical aspects of a situation. An influential twentieth-century view is Jerome Stolnitz's account of the "aesthetic attitude." For the details of these views, see DISINTEREST. See also, VALUE OF ART. For a criticism of disinterest, see PHENOMENOLOGY, BOURDIEU.

Further Reading

Beardsley, M. C. (1970), "The aesthetic point of view," in H. E. Kiefer and M. K. Munitz (eds), *Contemporary Philosophic Thought*, vol. 3. Albany: State University of New York Press, pp. 219–37.

Bullough, E. (1912), " 'Psychical distance' as a factor in art and an aesthetic principle." *British Journal of Psychology*, 5: 87–98.

Carroll, N. (2001), "Four concepts of aesthetic experience," in his *Beyond Aesthetics: Philosophical Essays*. Cambridge: Cambridge University Press.

Dickie, G. (1964), "The myth of the aesthetic attitude." *American Philosophical Quarterly*, 1.1: 56–65.

Ingarden, R. (1973), *The Cognition of the Literary Work of Art*, R. A. Crowley and K. R. Olsen (trans.). Evanston: Northwestern University Press.

Stolnitz, J. (1960), *Aesthetics and Philosophy of Art Criticism*. Boston: Riverside.

Aesthetic Judgment

An aesthetic judgment (a.k.a., a judgment of taste) is a judgment that a work of art is good, beautiful, powerful, and so on. Strictly speaking, the term should be reserved for judgments that are grounded on aesthetics-centered views of art; some philosophers believe that the nature and value of art do not turn on aesthetics (see DEFINING ART, ADORNO, DANTO, DICKIE, HEIDEGGER). (For a survey of some grounds of evaluation that do not turn on the aesthetic, see VALUE OF ART.)

There are a number of old adages that advance the notion that aesthetic judgments are subjective: "Beauty is in the eye of the beholder," "There's no disputing taste," "One man's trash is another man's treasure." Perhaps such a view seems unproblematic in relation to taste and judgments of foods, beverages, and so on; I do not resist the claim that my distaste for curry is a mere personal preference.

But when I assert that Van Gogh's *The Bridge at Trinquetaille* (1888) is beautiful, is good art, or that The Pied Piper's version of Johnny Mercer's "Dream" (1945) is aesthetically pleasing, I do resist the claim that I am merely stating a subjective, personal preference. In other words, I am prepared to argue about it, to provide reasons to support my conclusion. The fact that I take this tack shows that I intend my judgment not to be merely subjective. Such observations are taken to show that, at least initially, we tend to understand aesthetic judgments as more than mere subjective preferences. We then turn to aesthetic theories to substantiate this position.

The two key figures to consider on the traditional notion of aesthetic judgment are David HUME and Immanuel KANT. Neither philosopher believes that BEAUTY (or the aesthetic) is a quality of objects. Notice that if it were, an aesthetic judgment would be a simpler matter; it would primarily involve looking to see if the object in question possesses the quality at issue. In the eighteenth century, philosophers began to argue that beauty, the aesthetic, and thus evaluations of works of art, involve a *reaction* on the part of a spectator; beauty is defined in a way that depends upon a sense for beauty, taste.

Both Hume and Kant acknowledge that aesthetic judgments are based on *subjective* experiences of pleasure, yet these judgments are put forward as stronger than mere subjective opinions or preferences. Hume sets out to find a standard of taste by means of which to make sense of this claim to objectivity (or something close to it). Hume claims that a "standard of taste" can be found in the consensus of experts ("true judges") whom we can identify via *their* qualities. The kinds of qualities that matter in such a critic are perceptual acuity, familiarity with many works of art, experience in judging many works of art, good sense, lack of prejudice, and so on (for more detail about this view, see HUME, "OF THE STANDARD OF TASTE"). Kant's view is very different. To put it in very simple terms, the objectivity of aesthetic judgments rests on the fact we all have the same kind of perceptual-cognitive apparatus. The point is not that we all cognize and perceive with the same precision but that our mental equipment is basically the same. When I perceive something in a certain manner (DISINTERESTEDLY), and if the object has certain FORMAL qualities, it sends the perceptual and cognitive components of my mind into a pleasing, harmonious relation—this pleasing feeling is the ground of aesthetic judgment. (For more detail, and the Kantian terminology, see KANT, THE CRITIQUE OF JUDGMENT.)

An interesting line of criticism directed against traditional accounts of aesthetic judgment and taste is sociopolitical in nature. MARXISTS, and those influenced by that tradition, often maintain that the judgments and principles of taste deemed objective on the traditional view are not objective at all; rather, such norms of taste are a mere creation of culture, a product of sociopolitical forces. Pierre BOURDIEU, for example, criticizes Kant's view specifically: "Kant's analysis of the judgment of taste finds its real basis in a set of aesthetic principles which are the universalization of the dispositions associated with a particular social and economic condition" (Bourdieu, 1984, p. 493). Bourdieu's criticism has political implications; he claims that taste is used by the bourgeoisie as a tool of domination. See ADORNO, BENJAMIN.

Further Reading

Bourdieu, P. (1984 [1979]), *Distinction: A Social Critique of the Judgement of Taste*, R. Nice (trans.). Cambridge, MA: Harvard University Press.

Korsmeyer, C. (2005), "Taste," in D. M. Lopes and B. Gaut (eds), *The Routledge Companion to Aesthetics*. London and New York: Routledge Press.

Zangwill, N. (2010), "Aesthetic Judgment," in E. Zalta (ed.), *The Stanford Encyclopedia of Philosophy* (Winter 2012 edn). http://plato.stanford. edu/entries/aesthetic-judgment

Aesthetic Properties

(Aesthetic properties are occasionally referred to as aesthetic *qualities*.) A painting may be BEAUTIFUL, ugly, garish, or balanced; a piece of music may be joyful, clumsy, powerful, or somber. These are what some philosophers have called AESTHETIC properties. Contrast these properties with others that are considered nonaesthetic: a painting may weigh five pounds, it may be rectangular, or it may consist of mostly blues and greens; a piece of music may be 20 minutes long, or it may be in the key of C. Aesthetic properties do not form a homogeneous group; notice, for example, that a property such as joyousness is emotive (see EMOTION) whereas a property such as balance is a FORMAL property. Some philosophers deny that there is a distinction at all between aesthetic and nonaesthetic properties (Ted Cohen, for example). Following Frank SIBLEY, the discussion occasionally turns on "aesthetic *concepts*," where the issue is couched in terms of correct or incorrect application of one or another aesthetic concept to a work of art; for example, if a work of art is not graceful, it would be incorrect to apply the aesthetic concept *gracefulness* to it. There is disagreement over the nature of aesthetic properties and their relationships to other phenomena and issues. However, to attain an initial lay of the land, we can consider aesthetic properties to be the constituents of AESTHETIC EXPERIENCES (perhaps perceiving an aesthetic property is the fruit of adopting the perceptual comportment of DISINTEREST, the aesthetic attitude). Further, aesthetic properties can serve as foundations for AESTHETIC JUDGMENTS; after all, to describe a painting as graceful is already to imply that it is good in one sense or another; to describe a painting as clumsy is to imply the opposite. Along these lines, Monroe BEARDSLEY calls aesthetic properties "value-grounding qualities." (See VALUE OF ART.)

Determining whether a work of art possesses certain nonaesthetic properties such as those mentioned above seems straightforward; determining whether a work of art possesses certain aesthetic properties is anything but. Frank Sibley maintains that perceiving aesthetic properties requires taste. The idea is that a person without taste may easily see that a painting contains curved lines but will not apprehend its gracefulness. Aesthetic properties are, in some sense, dependent upon a work of art's nonaesthetic properties; however, according to Sibley, although a particular aesthetic property may depend for its existence upon one or another nonaesthetic property, we cannot infer from nonaesthetic properties the existence of particular aesthetic properties. Kendall WALTON points out that the aesthetic properties one perceives a work of art to have do not depend merely upon a work's nonaesthetic properties. Aesthetic properties depend also upon the art category to which the work belongs (performance art, visual art, conceptual art, music, and so on). Perceiving a work of art as belonging in one category may lead to perceiving some aesthetic properties that I would not perceive were I to conceive of it as belonging to another category.

The old adage, "beauty is in the eye of the beholder," suggests that beauty, and perhaps other aesthetic properties, is subjective; what you find to be poignant, I may not. While it is surely true that aesthetic properties are not objective in the sense that the mind-independent properties of physics are (mass, for instance), aesthetic properties do not seem to be entirely subjective (like a pain, for instance). Aesthetic properties seem to be more like colors, which are observable, response-dependent properties, so-called *secondary qualities* (see BEAUTY for early versions of this view). Notwithstanding colorblind persons, perceivers agree about which objects are green, aqua, and so on. So, perhaps aesthetic properties are as objective and as real as color properties. That said, although some people may agree about which works of art possess which aesthetic properties, there seems to be much more variation in the attribution of aesthetic properties than the attribution of color properties.

David HUME worried about the possibility that even experts ("true judges") may disagree on matters of taste, due to cultural differences and differences of temperament. Continental and feminist philosophers typically contend that different cultures, social classes, and genders do not necessarily share notions of beauty, taste, and other aesthetic properties. Pierre BOURDIEU, for example, claims that the traditional notion of the aesthetic (Immanuel KANT'S) is not a universal aesthetic but merely a description of an upper class aesthetic. See FEMINIST CRITIQUE.

Further Reading

Cohen, T. (1973), "Aesthetic/non-aesthetic and the concept of taste." *Theoria*, 39: 113–52.

Goldman, A. (2009), "Aesthetic properties," in S. Davies, K. M. Higgins, R. Hopkins, R. Stecker, and D. E. Cooper (eds), *A Companion to Aesthetics*. Oxford: Wiley-Blackwell.

Kivy, P. (1973), *Speaking About Art*. The Hague: Martinus Nijhoff.

Arousal of Emotion, see Expression

Beauty

G. W. F. HEGEL held that the subject matter of the philosophy of art is beauty. This accurately reflects the traditional importance of the concept in our subfield. Charles Batteux, in 1747, defines art as "the imitation of beautiful nature" (see the introduction and REPRESENTATION). However, beauty has become increasingly marginalized in the philosophy of art during the last 200 years. In common parlance, we call many things beautiful in addition to works of art; in fact, almost anything can be called beautiful: a work of art, an idea, an action, a natural object, a person, and so on. Traditionally, going back to the ancient Greeks, beauty is closely associated with the good, the fine, the noble, the divine, and truth. Beauty is also typically associated with praise, in general, and it is nearly universally thought to be a source of pleasure. It is unsurprising, then, that when we call something beautiful, we simultaneously intend a positive evaluation. Some philosophers have set out to pull apart these notions. In his unpublished notes, collected as *The Will to Power,* Friedrich NIETZSCHE writes, "For a philosopher to say, 'the good and the beautiful are one,' is infamy; if he goes on to add, 'also the true,' one ought to thrash him. Truth is ugly" (1968, p. 429).

Setting Nietzsche aside, this broad notion of the beautiful approximates the scope of the meaning of the corresponding ancient Greek term, *tò kalón.* The familiar notion that beautiful things are ordered, harmonious, and proportional is traceable to the Greek Pythagorean tradition; it is influential in the later Greek tradition, in the Middle Ages, and so on. In his *Philebus,* PLATO characterizes beauty as involving measure and proportion. In the *Symposium,* he is primarily concerned with beauty in relation to love, and he discusses absolute beauty, a *form* of beauty (just as he maintains that there is a form of justice, or more similarly, The Good). Like Plato's other forms, absolute beauty is eternal, unchanging, mind-independent, immaterial, ideal, and not knowable through perception but knowable only through the intellect (notice how counterintuitive the claim is that beauty is not knowable through perception). Beautiful things, such as works of art, individuals, and flowers, are beautiful only imperfectly, and they are beautiful only insofar as they *partake* in absolute beauty. While Plato praises beauty, he is famously critical of the arts, on epistemic, moral, psychological, and political grounds; see PLATO, *REPUBLIC.*

Aristotle takes beauty to be a property of works of art, which is due to their proportion, order, and so on. For example, a beautiful tragic drama has a plot that is unified, possessing a beginning, middle, and end, in addition to other features (see ARISTOTLE,

POETICS). The Stoics maintain that beauty is a matter of symmetry. The neoplatonic philosopher Plotinus counters this in the claim that even simple sense qualities can be beautiful.

Francis Hutcheson (1694–1746) holds that beauty is not a quality that certain objects possess. Rather, beauty is an "idea" (a mental object, in John Locke's sense). Certain objects have the power or disposition to cause in us the idea of beauty. The objects that possess this power have parts that bear a certain relation to one another; this relation is, in Hutcheson's famous phrase, "uniformity amidst variety." In short, objects that display uniformity amid variety are called beautiful because those objects cause in us the idea of beauty. We experience this idea of beauty, and the pleasure of beauty, immediately, not due to our external senses (sight or touch, for instance) but due to a special internal sense of beauty. The pleasure of beauty is purely sensible, and does not involve reason. David HUME, whom Hutcheson influenced, did not specify what it is that objects we call beautiful possess, and he believed that reason is, indeed, involved in much the way it is involved in his moral theory (see HUME, "OF THE STANDARD OF TASTE").

For Immanuel KANT, beauty in NATURE outstrips beauty in art. He maintains that we cannot define beauty in terms of qualities of objects (such as proportion, order, balance, and so on). There are simply no principles of beauty. But we certainly do find objects to be beautiful. If we cash this out in terms of a mere approving *reaction* to an object, beauty will turn out to be nothing but a subjective preference; the proverb will be proven true, "beauty is in the eye of the beholder." Kant does focus on our reaction, our experiences of beauty, but he also focuses on our judgments of beauty (also known as judgments of taste), and in doing so, attempts to sidestep the problem of subjectivity. Kant maintains that when we experience an object that we deem beautiful . . . (1) we take pleasure in the object *for its own sake*; this is what Kant calls DISINTERESTED pleasure. That is, we do not have an interest in the object's existence nor in possessing the object. This distinguishes the beautiful from the gratifying (e.g., a sweet-tasting food), the practical, and the moral. (2) We recognize that this is not merely a subjective preference; we expect that others will find the object to be beautiful as well (even though there is no conceptual justification for this expectation). (3) The pleasure in the object is due to the object's FORM; in addition, we experience the object as not having an objective purpose but "merely formal purposiveness," or "purposiveness without purpose"; the purposiveness it does have has to do with the efficacy of its form. (4) We expect that others *should* find the object to be beautiful (see CREATIVITY). For philosophers after Kant and Hegel, especially in the twentieth century, beauty becomes a less central issue. Many have emphasized the broader notion of the AESTHETIC. We often value works of art AESTHETICALLY that we would not consider to be beautiful, such as an art installation consisting of garbage or a song in the rock genre of psychobilly. In the twentieth century, beauty comes to be seen as one AESTHETIC PROPERTY among others, albeit a central one. However, with the advent of the avant-garde, works of art are often valued that are neither beautiful nor aesthetic. Recently, interest in beauty has re-emerged; see, for example, Mary Mothersill (1984) and Arthur Danto (2003).

Further Reading

Danto, A. C. (2003), *The Abuse of Beauty: Aesthetics and the Concept of Art*. Chicago and La Salle: Open Court.

Hutcheson, F. (1973), *An Inquiry Concerning Beauty, Order, Harmony, Design*, P. Kivy (ed.). The Hague: Martinus Nijoff.

Mothersill, M. (1984), *Beauty Restored*. Oxford: Oxford Clarendon Press.

—(2009), "Beauty," in S. Davies, K. M. Higgins, R. Hopkins, R. Stecker, and D. E. Cooper (eds), *A Companion to Aesthetics*. Oxford: Wiley-Blackwell.

Nietzsche, F. (1968), *The Will to Power*, W. Kaufmann and R. J. Hollingdale (trans.). New York: Vintage.

Catharsis

The philosopher most associated with the notion of catharsis is Aristotle; he discusses catharsis in his *Poetics* and *Politics*. In ancient Greek, *katharsis* refers to cleansing or purification. In what seems to be a response to Plato's critical point that poetry spurs the emotions to the detriment of a spectator's well-being, Aristotle holds that tragic poetry's arousal of the emotions is therapeutic. The emotions most associated with tragedy are pity and fear;

the arousal of these emotions purges or vents these (and perhaps similar, destructive) emotions. The thought is that, unpurged, these emotions can be psychologically disruptive. This is the traditional interpretation of Aristotle's view. According to Aristotle, catharsis is the purpose (telos) of tragedy. According to another interpretation, catharsis is taken to be educative; the emotions of pity and fear are clarified or calibrated. Through aesthetic experiences, a spectator learns when it is appropriate to experience an emotion such as pity, to what degree, in relation to which actions and situations, and so on. For more about the philosophical context in which catharsis emerges, see PLATO, *REPUBLIC*; ARISTOTLE, *POETICS*. Also see EMOTIONS, TRAGEDY.

Further Reading

Aristotle (1986), *The Poetics of Aristotle*, S. Halliwell (trans.). London: Duckworth.
—(2000), *Politics*, B. Jowett (trans.). New York: Dover Publications.
Lear, J. "Katharsis," in A. Rorty (ed.), *Essays on Aristotle's Poetics*. Princeton: Princeton University Press, 1992.

Censorship

Censorship is a POLITICAL issue in the sense that it has to do with the freedom of expression, which ultimately has to do with political freedom in general. History is littered with attempts by political leaders and other authorities to prohibit or restrict access to works of art that convey ideas and emotions deemed dangerous in one way or another. Some works of art are thought to be morally dangerous (cases in which authorities find a work of art to be, e.g., obscene). Some works of art are thought to be religiously dangerous (cases in which authorities find a work of art to be blasphemous). Some works of art are thought to be politically dangerous (cases in which authorities find a work of art's content to conflict with the dominant ideology), and so on.

Consider three examples of censorship. In the United States, the First Amendment of the Constitution protects free speech, which is taken to include artistic expression, but in recent decades, Congress has placed pressure on the National Endowment for the Arts not to fund obscene—later amended to "indecent"—works of art. This may be better described as indirect censorship. Salman Rushdie's controversial novel, *The Satanic Verses* (1988), was banned in a number of countries. More outrageously, Iran's Ayatollah Ruhollah Khomeini issued a fatwa, calling upon Muslims to murder Rushdie. Such threats have a negative affect beyond the country in which a work of art is banned because they encourage artists to self-censor. In the 1940s and the 1950s, the US Congress's House Un-American Activities Committee investigated a number of Hollywood screenwriters, actors, and directors seeking to discover who in Hollywood had communist ties. The committee's Cold-War-motivated concern was that some Hollywood films had, and would continue to have, procommunist or anti-American themes. The so-called "Hollywood Ten" were a group under investigation, who refused to cooperate, and challenged the committee's constitutionality. They were cited for contempt of Congress, each was sentenced to one year in prison, and they were subsequently unable to work in Hollywood; they—and others—were blacklisted.

If art is particularly worrisome to authority figures, political groups, and so on, it is largely for a reason Plato identified more than 2,000 years ago: artists do not simply communicate ideas (see REPRESENTATION), they make ideas *appealing*; artists do this in part by trafficking in the emotions, and by utilizing enticing features of art such as rhythm, rhyme, melody, color, and so on (see PLATO, REPUBLIC). One way in which philosophers have responded to such criticism, especially FORMALISTS, is to argue that art's content (including its moral content) is relevant neither to the understanding of works of art nor the evaluation of works of art *qua* art. Another way in which to defend art is to argue that artistic expression is a kind of free speech; one can then appeal to one or another defense of free speech (for a more detailed account of these defenses, and additional further readings, see ETHICS).

Further Reading

Hoffman, B. (1998), "Censorship," in M. Kelly (ed.), *Encyclopedia of Aesthetics* (four volumes). New York and Oxford: Oxford University Press.

Williams, B. (2009), "Censorship," in S. Davies, K. M. Higgins, R. Hopkins, R. Stecker, and D. E. Cooper (eds), *A Companion to Aesthetics*. Oxford: Wiley-Blackwell.

Conceptual Art

Influenced by artists such as Marcel Duchamp and John Cage, the conceptual art movement emerged in the 1960s, through the work of artists such as Joseph Kosuth and Sol LeWitt. Although Duchamp's ready-mades and other works of art that preceded this movement posed challenges to traditional philosophy of art, conceptual art puts a fine point on these challenges. The principal feature of conceptual works of art is the idea, conception, or meaning. Conceptual artists de-emphasize the perceivable object, the physical medium, in favor of the idea. In fact, in some cases, a material medium is entirely absent. This cuts against the traditional notion that the work of artists is embodied in a medium—in paint, sounds, words, clay, and so on. Moreover, this cuts against the tradition that engaging with a work of art requires directly perceiving that object.

Since the ideas that anchor conceptual works are often imperceptible, conceptual works of art can be perceptually indistinguishable from ordinary objects. Consequently, a definition of art that accommodates conceptual art will have to define art in terms of nonmanifest properties. One definition that accomplishes this is Arthur DANTO'S, which, in part, maintains that works of art are necessarily *about* something, and they express a point of view about their meaning. Notice that such features can be nonmanifest. Another relevant definition is George DICKIE'S institutional theory of art, which states that art status is conferred upon an artifact by a certain *procedure*, which is grounded in the social practices of an artworld (see DEFINING ART).

What kind of thing is a conceptual work of art? Regarding traditional painting, a physical ONTOLOGY seems viable; at least at first blush, a painting seems to be a physical thing, the painted canvas. This seems less viable regarding conceptual art. Perhaps a conceptual work of art is a type, as musical works or literary works are often thought to be. An idealist ontology, such as R. G. COLLINGWOOD'S, takes works of art to be ideas, mental entities. Although an idealist ontology is generally subject to effective criticisms, it seems less problematic regarding conceptual art, given its emphasis on the idea. David Davies has recently suggested that conceptual works are not things but actions—action-*tokens* (rather than action-types, as Gregory Currie maintains).

Since we do not directly perceive conceptual works of art, some traditional notions of the VALUE OF ART are rendered implausible. For example, it seems that the value of conceptual art cannot rest upon the affordance of AESTHETIC EXPERIENCE, at least as traditionally conceived. Does this serve as a general reason to reject aesthetic definitions of art, or is it a reason to resist the claim that conceptual art is truly art? The dominant view of the value of conceptual art is cognitivist in nature; conceptual works of art are valued for the ideas that constitute them; these works are intended to make one think. We do not engage with perceptual features, but rather ideas. This notion of value highlights an aspect of the challenge in defining art: art that is idea-centered must be distinguished from other idea-centered endeavors such as philosophy. The definitions mentioned above each address this challenge in their own way.

Further Reading

Currie, G. (1988), *An Ontology of Art*. New York: St Martin's Press.
Davies, D. (2004), *Art as Performance*. Malden, MA: Blackwell.
Goldie, P. and Schellekens, E. (eds) (2007), *Philosophy and Conceptual Art*. Oxford: Oxford University Press.

Creativity

It was not lost on the ancients that artists were up to something valuable and seemingly inexplicable; artists were thought to be inspired by Muses. In Homer's *Odyssey*, we find passages to this effect: "The Muse stirred the singer to sing the famous actions of men on that venture, whose fame goes up into the wide heaven" (2009, VIII, 70). And later in book VIII, Odysseus says, " 'For with all peoples upon earth singers are entitled to be cherished and to their share of respect, since the Muse has taught them her own way, and since she loves all the company of singers.' " (2009, VIII 475).

Similarly, PLATO argues that unlike experts in crafts (*technai*), such as medicine or carpentry, whose work consists of skilled activity that can be taught and explained by appeal to principles, for artists, skill is not enough. Artists work through divine inspiration; while creating, artists are not in control. Thus, credit for creative works rests primarily in the source of inspiration rather than in the artist, who is a mere vehicle (see Plato's *Phaedrus* and *Ion*). Much later, the psychologist Sigmund Freud (1856–1939) suggested that repressed thoughts occupy something like the role performed above by divine inspiration.

According to Immanuel KANT, creating art requires an innate capacity he calls genius, which provides the material for art ("aesthetic ideas") and enables the artist to do more than merely follow rules. In this sense, creativity is inexplicable; it cannot be conceptualized. But artists must also cultivate the skills to develop an original idea according to the standards of taste. Only by means of both genius and the cultivation of talent does a work of art become beautiful. G. W. F. HEGEL claims that Kant's criteria for success are too individualistic and subjective. The historical context that determines whether or not a work of art is valuable or successful is not only an individual assessment of the artist's taste but an assessment of the work of art's success in conveying its culture's values (the culture's notion of freedom); thus, there is a restriction on art's content.

A familiar picture of the nature of the creative process is that it is a kind of EXPRESSION. The artist experiences an emotion which she is driven to express in a work of art. According to Leo Tolstoy's version of expression theory, the artist is actually experiencing the emotion while she is creating; the artist's desire to embody the emotion in paint, words, sound, and so on, leads to the emotion serving as a guide in the creative process. For Tolstoy, the ultimate goal is communication; it is a central part of his theory that the same emotion be aroused in spectators. Tolstoy's critics have pointed out that when an artist puts pen to paper, to express in a work of art an extreme emotion such as misery, it is unlikely that she is actually miserable while carrying out the complex work involved in writing a novel or composing music. It is more likely, as Suzanne Langer (1895–1985) suggests, that artists *imagine* an emotion (drawing upon their knowledge of emotions), which then governs their various decisions (see DANCE).

A different kind of expression theory was put forward by R. G. COLLINGWOOD. He holds that artistic creativity is not a matter of mere skill or technique, and it does not transpire by beginning with a preconceived plan that is subsequently executed, such as the plan to arouse emotions or the plan to imitate an object in nature (see REPRESENTATION). Collingwood maintains that art turns on the expression of emotions but not with an aim to arouse the emotion in spectators. The creative process begins with an inchoate emotion, a "perturbation or excitement," which drives the artist to work. The artist is oppressed by this emotion, an oppression which is eased by working. Through the creative process of imaginative expression—guided by this germ of an emotion—the process clarifies the emotion, renders it intelligible. The emotion only becomes conscious in expression. One especially thought-provoking aspect of his view is that the creative process serves as a kind of self-discovery. (See COLLINGWOOD, *PRINCIPLES OF ART*.)

Collingwood's view is an example of what Monroe BEARDSLEY refers to as "the propulsive theory of creation." Another common notion of creativity conceives of it as a kind of *problem-solving*. This is to be contrasted with the propulsive view in that a problem comes first; solving the problem is presented as a kind of goal at the outset. This fits what Beardsley calls the "finalistic" or "goal-directed" view of artistic creation. Beardsley considers, and criticizes, David Ecker's view, which suggests that the creative process involves stages of problems and solutions. The problems are not formulated linguistically but are presented in an art form's medium. In working toward his own view, Beardsley draws a useful distinction between two phases of creation. He suggests that there is an inventive phase, during which new ideas are formed and appear, and a selective phase, which involves self-criticism and editing. Beardsley concludes that understanding the artist's process is not relevant to our understanding or appreciating a work of art. The relevant creativity occurs in the work itself and in the spectator's experience of it. This jibes with Beardsley's early writing on the intentional fallacy (the view that an artist's intentions are not relevant to the understanding and interpretation of literary works of art). (See INTERPRETATION.) Along these lines, with an emphasis on evaluation, John Hospers (1918–2011) asserts, "the merits of a work of art must be judged by what we can find in the work of art, quite regardless of the conditions under which the work of art came into being. Its genesis is strictly irrelevant; what we must judge is the work before us, not the process of the artist who created it" (1954–55, p. 147).

Turning away from the process, we can ask what makes an idea or artifact a product of creativity? Margaret A. Boden (b. 1936) claims that products of creativity must be new, but *more* than new— after all, the can of Diet Coke on my desk is new—but it must also be *surprising*. This captures a part of what we mean when we call something innovative, novel, fresh, or unique. But even being new and surprising is not enough for something to be considered creative. Notice that a sentence may be new, and surprising, but many such sentences are not considered creative. Boden also emphasizes that creative things are valuable; this captures more of what we mean by calling something original, and so on. Note that whether one takes a work of art to be valuable will depend upon which account of the VALUE OF ART one accepts. Some accounts of art's value will take creativity to be irrelevant to art's value (as above); according to FORMALISM, for instance, creativity is irrelevant to artistic value because artistic value is a matter of a work of art's form alone.

Boden also draws a distinction between *psychological* creativity and *historical* creativity. An idea or artifact is creative in the first sense when it is new merely to the creator but has been done before. An idea is creative in the historical sense when it is new to the creator and new in history. This points to an important issue in the arts; a work of art can only be novel against the background of an art form's tradition. These relations to a context are what make it possible for a work of art to be treated as original or for it to be influential (recall Hegel's criticism of Kant above). (Also see DANTO, DICKIE.)

For Martin HEIDEGGER, works of art contain a deep originality that extends well beyond the work of art—works of art create conditions of intelligibility; they create cultural paradigms. A Greek temple, for example, creates a background against which events and phenomena come to have the meaning they do for that culture. See HEIDEGGER, "THE ORIGIN OF THE WORK OF ART."

Further Reading

Beardsley, M. (1966), "On the creation of art." *Journal of Aesthetics and Art Criticism*, 25: 159–65. Cambridge University Press.

Boden, M. (1990), *The Creative Mind: Myths and Mechanisms.* New York: Basic Books.

Gaut, B. and Livingston P. (eds) (2007), *The Creation of Art: New Essays in Philosophical Aesthetics.* Cambridge University Press.

Homer (2009), *The Odyssey of Homer,* R. Lattimore (trans.). New York: HarperCollins.

Hospers, J. (1954–55), "The concept of artistic expression." *Proceedings of the Aristotelian Society,* 55: 313–44.

Criticism, see Aesthetic Judgment; Value

Defining *Art*

Lurking behind the quest for a definition of art is the VALUE OF ART; we want to know *what art is* because it is valuable to us. Many philosophers would emphasize, straightaway, that we need a definition that classifies without being honorific. In common parlance, when someone says something such as, "that figurine of Perry the Platypus is a work of art!" he typically intends to bestow value upon the figurine. Philosophers want to be able to determine which objects achieve art status without, at the same time, deeming them praiseworthy. Importantly, such a definition will provide the conceptual space for the existence of bad art (the alternative is to be able to distinguish only between things that are works of art and things that are not works of art).

Notice that art is not a natural kind; it cannot be defined or classified in the way scientists deal with water, tigers, and aluminum. This is why ONTOLOGY does not settle the definitional issue. Even if all works of art are one kind of thing (say, a physical thing), that kind is not unique to art, obviously. Moreover, the art forms seem ontologically multifarious; a painting seems to be a different kind of thing from a work of music, and perhaps they are both different from works of dance or performance art. Thus, if one sets out to answer the question, "what is art?" one will not offer a description of the natural kind *art* as an answer. Rather, art is a status that certain objects attain.

Philosophers' conception of art has not been static. There are two terms that are often associated with the arts in ancient Greek philosophy but neither of these terms functioned to define the arts as we know them today (the fine arts of painting, music, poetry, and so on). Both Greek terms refer also to other phenomena and activities that have little to do with the fine arts. One term is *mimēsis*, which means to imitate or copy. Regarding the arts, painters and poets represent their subject matter by imitating it, copying it; actors in a tragedy, for instance, represent individuals by copying their actions; a painting of a horse depicts a horse insofar as it looks like a horse. But many other, nonart activities also exemplify *mimēsis*; for example, children's games often involve imitation. The Greeks also understood poetry, painting, music, and so on, as examples of *technē*, which is often translated as "art" or "craft." But carpentry, medicine, and generalship are also *technai* (the plural form of the term); these are obviously skills that we now take to be quite different from the fine arts. More specifically, a *technē* is any skillful practice based on rational principles. Also problematically, the Greeks understood some *technai* to be related to others for different reasons; we find, for example, that in some respects, music is taken to be more similar to mathematics than to painting.

A conception of art more familiar to us began to emerge in the eighteenth century. On this view, what we now understand to be the arts are considered a unique group: poetry, painting, sculpture, music, theater, dance, and architecture (subsequently, photography, film, and others have been added)—these are the fine arts, *les beaux arts* (see the introduction). At this time, philosophers began posing the question—"What is art?" That is, they began wondering about what makes the objects and activities in that group unique—what makes something a work of art? This is not to seek a definition of the English word "art," but rather to seek a definition of the concept, *art*.

This question, "What is art?" is similar to questions such as "What is a bachelor?" The latter question is effectively answered by providing a definition of the concept, *bachelor*. According to the most basic definition, a bachelor is simply an unmarried man. Now, imagine that you have been given the admittedly bizarre assignment of sorting a number of very androgynous people into a group of bachelors and another group of nonbachelors. The first person walks up; you ask, "Are you a man?" He says that he is. You then ask, "Are you unmarried?" He is unmarried. You classify this person as a bachelor. You would not classify a woman as a bachelor because it is a *necessary condition* for being a bachelor that a person be male. Similarly, it is a necessary condition for being a bachelor that a person be unmarried. Satisfying both of these conditions (being male and unmarried) is unique to bachelors; in other words, taken together, these are *sufficient conditions* for being a bachelor (these conditions are jointly sufficient). The concept, *bachelor,* is clarified by its definition. Unpacking a concept into its necessary and sufficient conditions is what is called conceptual analysis, which is exactly what analytic philosophers do, according to one characterization of analytic philosophy (see the introduction).

Many philosophers have tried to analyze the concept *art* so as to yield a definition like the one above; they have sought necessary and sufficient conditions for a thing's being art. This sort of definition is called an *essential definition*, or a *real definition*. Imagine how useful it would be to have such a definition. In addition to your ability to sort bachelors from nonbachelors, you would have the amazing ability to distinguish art from nonart. You may have already attempted something like this, based on your intuitions alone, upon encountering a particular installation (say) in an art gallery; you may have declared—"*That* is not art!"

A number of theories highlight a single function or property that is purported to be unique to art. Although he explicitly limits himself to visual art, this approach is epitomized by Clive BELL's famous comment, "For either all works of visual art have some common quality, or when we speak of 'works of art' we gibber" (1914, ch 1). However, not all theories that have been *treated* as such were actually intended as essential definitions. Some theories that have been interpreted as failed attempts at definition were put forward more generally as ways of understanding art and its value. For example, since philosophers writing prior to the eighteenth century conceived of art differently, it is a stretch to interpret them as attempting to define the modern concept of art. For example, we cannot interpret PLATO and ARISTOTLE as attempting to define art in our sense, even though they conceived of imitation as the key function of poetry, painting, and so on. Nevertheless, drawing upon such views, subsequent philosophers have floated imitation as the defining function of the modern conception of art: artifacts that serve the function of imitating—or more broadly, REPRESENTING— are works of art.

A number of other entries in this book describe views of art that have often been interpreted as attempts to provide an answer to this definitional question in terms of a single function or property: imitation theories suggest that works of art essentially copy or REPRESENT objects and events. Expression theories suggest that art's function is to *express* EMOTIONS (and in Leo Tolstoy's case, to arouse emotions as well). AESTHETIC theories suggest that art's function is to afford AESTHETIC EXPERIENCES. FORMALISM suggests that art possesses a special kind of form, which Clive BELL calls "significant form"; regarding music, Eduard Hanslick (1825–1904) calls music's special form "beautiful form." Two ways in which such definitions are commonly criticized is by noting (1) that there are artifacts that are commonly considered works of art that do *not* fulfill the function at issue (or do not possess the property), or (2) by noting that there are artifacts that do fulfill the function at issue (or do possess the property) that are *not* commonly considered works of art.

Is it even possible to define art? Ludwig Wittgenstein (1889–1951) maintains that certain abstract concepts lack essences. Famously, he suggests that one such concept is *game* (another is *sport*); *game* cannot be defined in terms of necessary and sufficient conditions; rather, the concept is defined in terms of a network of similarities, which Wittgenstein referred to as "family resemblances." Drawing from Wittgenstein, Morris Weitz (1916–81) suggests that art resists definition in that it is an open concept. Artists experiment and innovate in ways that expand the concept, violating any conception of art on offer (essentialism entails that art has an unchanging nature). Weitz puts forward the antiessentialist view that *art* is a family resemblance concept; there is no property or set of properties common to all works of art. That is, there are no necessary conditions for attaining art status, not even artifactuality (some works of art are simply natural objects). Works of art are classified as works of art insofar as they bear a family resemblance to one another. This view seems plausible when we consider the extreme variety objects and events that are considered works of art—are we to believe, for instance, that John Cage's musical work, *4' 33"*, and the Greek *Parthenon* have the same essential feature(s)? It has been argued against Weitz's view that works of art are, indeed, artifacts; an artist does something even to a natural object, in selecting it and presenting it as a work of art; this counts as artifactuality, which one can take then to be a necessary feature of works of art. Another criticism emerges from the question—how can we identify the salient resemblances, given that everything resembles everything else in one way or another? It also counts against Weitz's view that subsequent essential definitions of art made room for the requisite openness and innovation he emphasizes.

Any number of things considered art, according to the contemporary artworld, will fail to attain art status on traditional theories such as formalism or the expression theory. How can we understand the art-status of avant-garde art, such as ready-mades, CONCEPTUAL ART, and other art of the twentieth century? This challenge, as well as the shortcomings of previous theories, pressed philosophers toward different kinds of definitions. Arthur DANTO, writing about Andy Warhol's *Brillo Box* (1964), highlighted the fact that they are perceptually indistinguishable from the supermarket boxes that contain Brillo soap pads. Consequently, he reasoned, whatever makes *Brillo Box* a work of art must be due to nonexhibited properties. According to Danto, works of art are *about* something, they embody a meaning (*Brillo Box,* for instance, is about the nature of art). Further, works of art express a point of view about their meaning that requires INTERPRETATION. Importantly, an interpretation must be informed by the art theory that is appropriate to the work's location in history. The historical dimension of Danto's theory is central: accurately making sense of a work of art's meaning requires correctly identifying the art-historical context within which it was made. This role of the art-historical context in Danto's definition of art entails that a work of art such as *Brillo Box* could not have been a work of art in a period in which the theories are markedly different, for example, in the nineteenth century. Weitz's criticisms of essential definitions do not cut against Danto's theory, especially when Danto's "end of art" thesis is taken into consideration.

Danto's conception of an artworld had a significant influence upon George DICKIE'S institutional theory of art. Dickie offers a *procedural* definition of art. Art status is conferred upon an artifact by a certain *procedure* that is grounded in the social practices of an artworld. An artworld is a human institution consisting of artists, an art-going public, art schools, curators, critics, and so on. A work of art is an artifact that has the status of "candidate for appreciation" conferred upon (certain aspects of) it by someone acting on behalf of the artworld (usually, the artist). This is analogous to a member of the legal system (a judge, say) conferring marriage-status upon two people. Traditional kinds of works of art are artifacts in the normal sense: these are person-made objects. But Dickie also claims that ready-mades and found art are artifacts; artifactuality is conferred by a member of the artworld (for the second version of his theory, see DICKIE, GEORGE). Dickie's theory is classificatory only; it does not address art's VALUE. One criticism of the institutional theory of art is that if someone puts an artifact forward as a candidate for appreciation, she does so for a reason; *that reason*, critics say, is the important factor for art-status, not the social function performed by the artworld member.

More recently, philosophers have followed this trend of pursuing relational definitions of art that turn on art-historical, contextual relations. See, for example, Jerrold Levinson's "Defining art Historically" and "Refining Art Historically," in his *Music, Art, & Metaphysics*.

Further Reading

Bell, C. (1987 [1914]), *Art* (3rd edn). Oxford: Oxford University Press.
Davies, S. (1999), *Definitions of Art*. Ithaca, NY: Cornell University Press.
Dickie, G. (1984), *The Art Circle*. New York: Havens.
Levinson, J. (1990), *Music, Art, & Metaphysics: Essays in Philosophical Aesthetics*. Ithaca, NY: Cornell University Press.
Mandelbaum, M. (1965), "Family resemblances and generalization concerning the arts." *American Philosophical Quarterly*, 2: 219–28.
Weitz, M. (1956), "The role of theory in aesthetics." *Journal of Aesthetics and Art Criticism*,15: 27–35.
Wittgenstein, L. (1973 [1953]), *Philosophical Investigations* (3rd edn). G. E. M. Anscombe (trans.), Pearson.

Disinterest

A number of philosophers since the eighteenth century have claimed that there is a certain approach to art, a particular way of perceiving, which one must adopt in order to perceive art correctly; namely, an approach of disinterest, detachment, an "aesthetic attitude," "psychical distance." Such an approach is a necessary precondition for having an AESTHETIC EXPERIENCE. A notion of disinterest is developed by Immanuel KANT in his account of AESTHETIC JUDGMENT. He claims that when we judge something to be beautiful, we do so based on a certain kind of pleasurable experience, but the relevant sort of pleasure arises from a contemplative perception that is occupied with an object *for its own sake;* this is disinterested pleasure. This pleasure does not arise from an interest in the object's existing nor an interest in possessing it (thus, the pleasure grounding an aesthetic judgment is distinguished from mere agreeableness). Disinterest brackets the practical. According to Arthur SCHOPENHAUER, disengaging from practical concerns in aesthetic experience serves the additional, more profound purpose of providing an escape from the suffering that is at the core of human nature; in other words, aesthetic experiences temporarily disengage the individual will by bracketing our interests and desires. Note the profound VALUE OF ART on this view.

FORMALISTS encourage a kind of perceptual detachment. Clive BELL maintains that a work of art's REPRESENTATIONAL content is irrelevant to an artifact's art status. Consequently, in order to correctly perceive a work of art, one has to bracket that content, set it to one side. Eduard Hanslick (1825–1904) argues that music's expressing or arousing emotions is irrelevant to the essence of music, which rests in its structure. Therefore, in order to focus on the form, a careful listener will have to listen in a detached manner, so as to prevent emotions from being evoked as well as to disregard any emotions expressed or represented. Both theories conceive of art as autonomous, and instruct us to set aside heteronomous features.

Edward Bullough (1880–1934) holds that by putting "out of gear" the practical implications of a situation, we are able to perceive its aesthetic aspects; this is his notion of "psychical distance." For a passenger on a boat, a fog at sea may be practically problematic and fear-inducing, but considered at a psychical distance, its aesthetic qualities emerge, such as the interesting textures and shapes of things seen through the fog. There are various degrees of distance one can adopt vis-à-vis a work of art; a viewer must get this right; according to Bullough, a viewer can be too distant from a work of art.

Jerome Stolnitz offers an influential twentieth-century account of "the aesthetic attitude." He defines the aesthetic attitude as "disinterested and sympathetic attention to and contemplation of any object of awareness whatever, for its own sake alone" (1960, p. 35). In a critique of Stolnitz, George DICKIE denies the existence of this special, aesthetic mode of perception; he argues that failing to experience an object's aesthetic qualities is not due to adopting the wrong attitude but is due simply to attending to the wrong features of the object.

Consider a challenge to disinterest in general. Is it reasonable to accept that we perform perceptual tasks that involve being both passive and active? As Karen Hanson describes it—"actively finding the right psychical distance to let sensations be passively registered" (Hanson 2005, p. 563). More profound criticisms of disinterest come from philosophers who conceive of art as *essentially* intertwined with other dimensions of life. Regarding his emphasis on the connections between art and everyday life, consider John DEWEY; regarding cultural values, consider G. W. F. HEGEL; regarding politics, consider MARXISTS; regarding the body, consider Maurice Merleau-Ponty (see PHENOMENOLOGY). Such philosophers will balk at characterizing the perceptual approach to art as one that detaches art from these other dimensions of life. For an emphasis on the social situatedness of perception, and a direct critique of Kant's notion of disinterest, see BOURDIEU. Also see FEMINIST CRITIQUE, SUBLIME.

Further Reading

Bullough, E. (1912), " 'Psychical distance' as a factor in art and an aesthetic principle." *British Journal of Psychology*, 5: 87–98.
Dickie, G. (1964), "The myth of the aesthetic attitude." *American Philosophical Quarterly*, 1.1: 56–65.
Hanson, K. (2005), "Feminist Aesthetics," in D. M. Lopes and B. Gaut (eds), *The Routledge Companion to Aesthetics* (2nd edn). New York: Routledge Press.
Stolnitz, J. (1960), *Aesthetics and Philosophy of Art Criticism*. Boston: Riverside.

Emotion

If we construe emotion broadly to include not only the full-blown variety such as sadness and elation but also feelings such as pleasure, then we find emotion to be ubiquitous in the philosophy of art. PLATO maintains that many kinds of art are dangerous, due to art's ability to provoke the emotions, appealing to our irrational side, endangering the governing authority of one's reason. These and other worries led to his suggestion, in the REPUBLIC, to ban such works of art from his ideal society. More positively, ARISTOTLE claims that tragedy can have a therapeutic effect on spectators, by causing them to undergo catharsis, a purging or venting of emotions such as fear and pity and other potentially destructive emotions (for another interpretation, see ARISTOTLE, *POETICS*). AESTHETIC PROPERTIES such as BEAUTY are often considered to be essentially tied to feelings such as pleasure. AESTHETIC JUDGMENTS are traditionally thought to center on emotion, "sentiment" (see HUME, "*OF THE STANDARD OF TASTE*"). Even CLIVE BELL's influential FORMALISM turns on what he calls "the aesthetic emotion," which appears to be a kind of AESTHETIC EXPERIENCE.

However, there are also thinkers who believe that the emotions are exactly the wrong route to understanding works of art. Regarding the irrelevance of the arousal of emotions to this end, Eduard Hanslick (1825–1904), the musical formalist, writes, "Thus we say nothing at all concerning the crucial aesthetical principle of music if we merely characterize music in general, according to its effect upon feeling, just as little, perhaps, as we would get to know the real nature of wine by getting drunk" (1986, p. 6). One penetrating aspect of this criticism is that our emotional reactions to works of art are often idiosyncratic. (See MUSIC; FORMALISM.)

Certain theories of art, expression theories, take emotion to be central to art's nature and value (see DEFINING ART, VALUE OF ART). The puzzle has been to make sense of what it can mean to describe a painting or a piece of music as (say) melancholy. Clearly, works of art themselves do not possess psychological states; a painted canvas cannot be sad. Two common approaches have been to conceive of the emotions as the emotions of artists, which get expressed in their work, or, to conceive of the emotions as those aroused in spectators, readers, or listeners by engaging with the work.

The novelist Leo Tolstoy (1828–1910) outlines a straightforward expression theory of art in his *What Is Art?* (1898). Tolstoy's theory is often referred to as a "communication theory" because it rests on the idea that an artist communicates her emotions to spectators, readers, or listeners through her art. Tolstoy maintains that if an artifact is art, then the same emotion the artist puts into the work "infects" the spectator; that is, the work of art arouses that identical emotion in spectators. An important criterion for evaluating art, on Tolstoy's view, is that an artist's expression should be sincere. The value of art centers on its power to unify. As speech communicates ideas, art communicates emotions. As the ideas of others from this and past generations are accessible by means of speech, the emotions of others, present and past, are accessible through art. Art brings people together. Tolstoy claims that just as there is progress in ideas, there is progress in emotions; as time goes by, emotions that are not beneficial for mankind are discarded for those more beneficial. Which emotions are beneficial is judged in light of "the religious perception of the age." The best works of art transmit emotions consonant with such religious ideals.

Another influential expression theory is put forward by R. G. COLLINGWOOD in his PRINCIPLES OF ART. An important difference between Collingwood and Tolstoy is that, for Collingwood, artistic expression is a process through which the artist *clarifies* her emotion. (For Tolstoy, although it is important for an emotion to be clarified, it is fully formed prior to setting to work.) On Collingwood's view, the artist does not initially experience an emotion but rather "a perturbation or excitement," which drives her to work. This clarificatory expression is necessary and sufficient for art status; art is defined as an activity. Collingwood does not place importance on the arousal of emotions. Although Tolstoy claims that his notion of expression is to be distinguished from a mere venting or betraying of emotions (consider a baby crying, a yawn, or a temper tantrum), this distinction is emphasized in Collingwood's approach, given the stress he places on the process of clarification. This process of clarification is important for another reason as well; for Collingwood, this is a process of self-discovery. This is a dimension of the value of art not found in Tolstoy's theory.

Is the expression of emotion an effective way of defining art? Consider Tolstoy's view. The idea would be that artifacts that successfully express the emotion of the artist are works of art; communication is decisive; the spectator must be infected with the artist's emotion. Critics of this expression theory claim that the expression or arousal of emotions is not a *necessary* condition of art since we can identify indisputable examples of art that do not express or arouse emotions. And in addition, the expression or arousal of emotions is not a *sufficient* condition of art, since there are examples of actions that express or arouse emotions that are not works of art.

Consider two further problems with these theories. First, Tolstoy's theory renders works of art a mere means of communication. The communicated emotion can be identified independently of the work; whatever can express a given emotion is interchangeable with whatever else can express it (works of art, facial expressions, screams, et cetera). This renders the VALUE OF ART instrumental, which cuts against the common intuition that works of art are valued as ends in themselves. Second, both Tolstoy's and Collingwood's theories involve an artist experiencing the relevant emotion *during* the creative process (this is what it means for the artist to be sincere, on Tolstoy's view). This view of the creative process seems, to some philosophers, flawed. Consider a work of art that expresses an extreme form of misery; it is difficult to believe that while the artist is engaged in complex and challenging creative work she is actually undergoing that misery. More to the point, it is unlikely that artists can *only* create works with one emotional content or another while they are actually experiencing that emotion; artists do not seem to be so restricted by their occurrent feelings, emotions, and moods. Suzanne Langer (1895–1985) suggests that it is more likely that artists draw upon their *knowledge* of emotions; they do this in creating works of art that *symbolize* emotions (rather than expressing or arousing emotions). In other words, artists imagine a feeling, and this conception governs their work; such a conception of a feeling is what an artist presents through an artistic symbol. (Unlike linguistic symbols, which are discursive and referential, according to Langer, works of art are nondiscursive, presentational symbols.) See DANCE.

NELSON GOODMAN offers a theory of art as symbol, and a view of expression as metaphorical exemplification. A symbol that exemplifies does not refer by denoting but refers to one or more of the properties it possesses (for simplicity's sake, I am ignoring Goodman's nominalism here). Consider a tailor's swatch. While many items of clothing may be made of gabardine, a gabardine swatch is not only made of gabardine (possession), it also refers to gabardine; the swatch is the kind of symbol that exemplifies gabardine. Goodman claims that works of art express emotions and other properties by METAPHORICALLY exemplifying them. Works of art are often said to express emotions and other properties that they do not actually possess; for example, a piece of instrumental music may be said to express longing. Clearly, the piece of music itself is not literally longing for someone, but according to Goodman, the music can possess the property of longing *metaphorically*. Philosophers have come to accept that works of art can be *expressive of* emotions—works of art can possess expressive qualities—without being expressions of an artist's emotions (see Tormey 1971). It is not mysterious that novels, paintings, and sculptures can be expressive of emotions; for example, a writer (or a painter) can place a character in a novel (or a person depicted in a painting) in a frightening or melancholic situation. These are cases in which emotions, or the expressions of emotions, are REPRESENTED (more subtle are cases in which the emotions expressed are the narrator's). But what about art forms that do not represent characters, situations, events, and so on? How can a piece of instrumental music, for example, be expressive of emotion? Peter Kivy claims that a piece of music can be rightly characterized as sad (say) without its arousing sadness in a listener or expressing the sadness of a composer; instead, sad music is *expressive of* sadness. According to Kivy's "contour theory," music can be expressive of emotions such as sadness, sorrow, joy, fear, hope, etc. Just as cheerfulness is a property of the color yellow, sadness is a property of certain music. The emotion is an emergent, perceptual property that music possesses in virtue of the music's formal properties. Kivy takes a Saint Bernard's face to be an instructive analogy: it has particular, droopy features that make it look sad; sad music, similarly, has particular contours in virtue of which it sounds sad or melancholy (features of the music's form, such as a slow tempo and halting rhythm). A different sort of view was put forward by Jerrold Levinson (1996), who suggests that the emotions we hear in music are imaginatively attributed to a fictional *persona* in the music.

There are a number of puzzles about the relationship between emotions and art. In the case of so-called "negative emotions," such as fear and pity, why do we value engaging with works of art that express or arouse these emotions? Aristotle's catharsis provides one sort of answer. Another issue—how can we make sense of our experiencing emotions in relation to fictional characters and situations? See LITERATURE; DANCE; MUSIC; WALTON; ARISTOTLE, *POETICS*.

Further Reading

Davies, S. (1994), *Musical Meaning and Expression*. Ithaca and London: Cornell University Press.

Hanslick, E. (1986 [1854]), *On the Musically Beautiful*, G. Payzant (trans.). Indianapolis: Hackett.

Hospers, J. (1955), "The concept of artistic expression." *Proceedings of the Aristotelian Society*, 55: 313–44.

Kivy, P. (1989), *Sound Sentiment*. Philadelphia: Temple University Press.

Levinson, J. (1996). "Musical Expressiveness," in *The Pleasures of Aesthetics*. Ithaca, NY: Cornell University Press, pp. 90–125.

—(1997), "Music and negative emotion," in J. Robinson (ed.), *Music & Meaning*. Ithaca: Cornell University Press.

Tolstoy, L. (1930 [1898]), *What is Art?*, A. Maude (trans.). Oxford: Oxford University Press.

Robinson, J. M. (2007), *Deeper Than Reason: Emotion and Its Role in Literature, Music, and Art*. Oxford and New York: Clarendon Press.

Tormey, A. (1971), *The Concept of Expression*. Princeton, NJ: Princeton University Press.

Environmental Aesthetics, see Nature

Ethics

The consideration of the relationship between art and morality goes back to the very beginning of philosophical writing about art. One of the principal issues raised in this area is whether or not a work of art's moral content is relevant to its value *qua* art. An example of an assertion that it is, indeed, relevant is found in Leo Tolstoy's *What Is Art?* Although Tolstoy's book is often considered primarily as containing an EXPRESSION theory of art, he also claims that art should ultimately be valued on moral/religious grounds. Moral content is a principle criterion for evaluating art; good works of art, he claims, convey the moral/religious ideals of an age.

Is this right? Is the moral content of works of art relevant to their value *qua* art? Clearly, the subject matter of some works of art involves moral issues. Take Leni Riefenstahl's film, *Triumph of the Will* (1934), which depicts Hitler and the Nazi party in a very positive light. Consider Charlie Chaplin's *The Great Dictator* (1940), which lampoons them. Is the moral content of these films relevant to their artistic value? It is not a stretch to maintain that the Riefenstahl film is morally repugnant, but is that judgment about the moral content of the film, at the same time, a judgment against the work of art *qua* art? One can imagine Tolstoy maintaining that the subject matter of the Riefenstahl film is, indeed, a decisive strike against it.

FORMALISTS, aestheticists, and others have stressed art's autonomy. In his *ART*, the formalist Clive BELL holds that a work of art's form is the only aspect relevant to art status and value; all content (including moral content) is irrelevant. The related idea that experiences of works of art ought to be DISINTERESTED breaks off, as it were, the aesthetic realm from the practical, including the moral and political. It seems obvious to emphasize form in relation to instrumental music, abstract art, and other arts that seem to be light on content and heavy on form, so to speak. But these thinkers have also emphasized form and de-emphasized content in relation to other arts, even literature. An extreme version of this view is apparent in Oscar Wilde's (1854–1900) remark reflective of aestheticism, "There is no such thing as a moral or an immoral book. Books are well written or badly written. That is all" (Wilde 2005, p. 3). For our purposes, the shared point of these thinkers is that judging art in moral terms is to misunderstand art's value *qua* art.

These claims are disputable. In some cases, a work of art's moral message does seem to have something to do with its value *qua* art. For example, is it not the case that the positive moral value of the ideas floated John Lennon's "Imagine" (1971) has something to do with its value as a work of art? Isn't this also true of the Chaplin film mentioned above? Presenting such a cutting criticism of Hitler—in 1940—certainly seems to be relevant to the artistic value of the film. And isn't it difficult to heap too much praise upon the Riefenstahl film, given that it is unabashed Nazi propaganda? (Noël Carroll develops a view such as this in his "Moderate Moralism.")

If we go back farther in history, we find another concern about the relationship between art and morality, which is no less a concern today. Plato maintained that poetry and other arts can have a negative *effect* on a populace. For example, stories depicting the gods as possessing unethical character traits, as we occasionally find in Homer's *Iliad* and *Odyssey*, may have a negative effect upon the young. (This was no idle concern for Plato, as these poems were central components of children's education in ancient Athens.) Concerns about specific subject matter are deepened by Plato through the observation that the young cannot distinguish between direct statement and allegory. Even more troubling is the fact that art's formal characteristics (Plato explicitly considered rhythm and musical modes) have the power to make subject matter appealing, even in cases where it would not be appealing on its own. Again, regarding the young, Plato worried that a young person may find a work of art's content appealing, due to artistic devices, long before she can rationally assess its worth. It is important to note that underlying any such position is an appreciation of the power of art. Surely, Plato appreciated this power; he is known for employing artistic devices with great subtlety in his dialogues; in fact, he is considered by many to be the best writer in the history of philosophy (see PLATO, *REPUBLIC*).

Many works of art do possess potent subject matter. For example, Johann Wolfgang von Goethe's *The Sorrows of Young Werther* (1774) is thought to have led to a rash of suicides, imitative of the novella's protagonist. (Media-induced clusters of copycat suicides are now known as the "Werther Effect.") This concern is quite commonly discussed today, by politicians, social critics, and in the media generally. Violence in films and various genres of popular music are often cited as partial causes of heinous acts. For example, after the 1999 mass shooting at Columbine high school in Colorado, the public dialogue involved placing significant blame on the film *The Matrix* (1999), the rock band Judas Priest, and the musician Marilyn Manson for negatively influencing the Columbine shooters.

Although, there is often speculation about the behavioral effects of the arts after mass shootings and other such events, there appears to be no convincing evidence to support such claims. In his, "Art and Ethical Criticism: An Overview of Recent Directions of Research," Noël Carroll claims that "no one really possesses reliable knowledge of the relevant order of specificity concerning art's behavioral consequences, nor do we have any dependable means for predicting the regularly recurring pattern of social behavior that any work of art will elicit—either in the short or the long run—from normal viewers, listeners, and/or readers. Anyone who claims to have access to this information, as participants in this debate often do, is simply bluffing" (Carroll 2000, p. 356).

There is another approach open to philosophers for defending art with controversial moral content that falls outside societal norms. Philosophers can construe works of art as a type of free speech, and then invoke one or another defense of free speech. It is instructive to consider the philosopher John Stuart Mill's (1806–73) defense, which he offers in his *On Liberty* (1869). According to Mill, it is illegitimate for society to interfere with a person's actions (including speech) unless her actions directly harm another person's well-being (e.g., speech that directly incites violence). This is known as Mill's "harm principle." It is interesting that Mill does not argue in favor of free speech on the grounds that individuals have a natural *right* to free speech; rather—just as he argues for individual liberty in general—he rests his argument on *utility*; free speech is useful, beneficial to society. In his consideration of free speech, Mill points out that even assuming that a given opinion is false, it is useful to allow its free expression. He reasons that *knowing* the truth is not merely a matter of holding a belief as "dead dogma"; that is, even if the belief held is true, holding it unreflectively is not to possess knowledge. Therefore, even false beliefs are useful to a society, when expressed, because they provoke persons into reconsidering *why* they believe what they believe; the expression of opinions different from our own makes us think; it makes us consider (or reconsider) which reasons provide support for our beliefs. Free expression of even false opinions can transform dead dogma into knowledge. Perhaps even immoral art can be useful in this sense—it may help us to better understand immoral ideas; moreover, immoral art may remind us, or prompt us to think more deeply about why we hold the views we do. Note that even if this is a viable view, and a thought-provoking challenge to CENSORSHIP, it is a position about the *instrumental* VALUE OF ART, not its value *qua* art (see Carroll 2000 and Kieran 2005).

There is another question often raised about art and morality, and we have just brushed up against one kind of response to it. How effective are works of art in exploring and conveying moral issues? Works of art typically do not provide arguments or even supporting reasons for what we take to be their moral claims. In other words, works of art do not convey moral knowledge in terms of true, justified belief (this is similar to Plato's point about artists not having knowledge of the *forms*; see PLATO, *REPUBLIC*). However, even if this is true, some works of art do enable us to consider moral claims fleshed-out in concrete form, to discover connections between various moral issues, and to see moral experiments, as it were, carried out in a novel's characters and situations. This is to say that works of art can provide a vehicle for expanding one's moral imagination. In fact, works of art expand our imaginations in general. For such purposes, philosophers often use narratives in thought experiments; for example, the "Ring of Gyges" story in Plato's *Republic* is a thought experiment that encourages the reader to imagine cases that ultimately function as support for the claim that no one is just willingly.

By helping us to consider different points of view, works of art can also help us to think about moral issues pertaining to others— persons from other classes, of other ethnicities, and the other gender. Hegel takes art's primary role to be to convey a culture's moral values, as well as other aspects of its ethos. However, it is not easy to grasp how the more abstract art forms, such as instrumental music, dance, abstract visual art, and architecture, can possess moral content. See also VALUE OF ART; ADORNO.

Further Reading

Bermudez, J. and Gardner, S. (eds) (2002), *Art and Morality*. London: Routledge.

Carroll, N. (1996), "Moderate moralism." *British Journal of Aesthetics*, 36: 223–38.

—(2000), "Art and ethical criticism: An overview of recent directions of research." *Ethics*, 110: 2, 350–87.

Gaut, B. (2009), *Art, Emotion and Ethics*. Oxford: Oxford University Press.

Kieran, M. (2003), "Forbidden knowledge: The challenge of immoralism," in J. Bermúdez and S. Gardner (eds), *Art and Morality*. London: Routledge, pp. 56–73.

—(2005), "Art and morality," in J. Levinson (ed.), *The Oxford Handbook of Aesthetics*. Oxford and New York: Oxford University Press.

Lamarque, P. (1995), "Tragedy and moral value." *Australasian Journal of Philosophy*, 73: 239–49.

Levinson, J. (ed.) (1998), *Aesthetics and Ethics: Essays at the Intersection*. Cambridge: Cambridge University Press.

Mill, J. S. (2006 [1869]), *On Liberty*. New York and Boston: Pearson Longman.

Tolstoy, L. (1930 [1898]), *What is Art?*, A. Maude (trans.). Oxford: Oxford University Press.

Wilde, O. (2005), *The Picture of Dorian Gray and Other Writings*. New York: Simon & Schuster.

Expression

What is expression? Although one might consider the expression of an idea, a fact, and so on, regarding expression, philosophers of art are primarily concerned with the expression of EMOTIONS. In ordinary parlance, you may accept that crying expresses emotion, or throwing a temper tantrum, or perhaps even yawning. Philosophers of art have something else in mind. R. G. COLLINGWOOD and John DEWEY refer to crying, throwing a temper tantrum, and so on, as venting or betraying emotions rather than expressing them. Expression, properly construed, involves a thoughtful clarification or shaping of an emotion, shown-forth or embodied in paint, words, clay, and so on.

Clearly, many works of art involve the expression of emotions in one sense or another. Therefore, elucidating the phenomenon of the expression of emotions in art is a valuable endeavor. But the way in which expression often comes up is as a theory of art. By most counts, there are four traditional philosophical theories of art, each floating one or another property or function which they claim is essential to art: REPRESENTATION theory (imitation), FORMALISM, theories of AESTHETIC EXPERIENCE, and expression theory. (See DEFINING ART.) Of these four traditional theories, it is arguably expression theory that offers the best explanation of the motive to create art, as well as providing the most straightforward and convincing account of the VALUE OF ART.

The expression theory of art (in the hands of philosophers who aspire to formulate an essential definition of art) states that what makes a work of art a work of art is that it expresses emotions. Why would this be of value? Consider the novelist Leo Tolstoy's expression theory. Tolstoy holds that just as speech communicates ideas, art *communicates* emotions. An artist, while experiencing an emotion, embodies this emotion in her work. In successful cases, a spectator is "infected" by the emotion. Art is valuable due to this expressive capacity and its ability to unify people by means of such works. Notice that conceiving of art on this model emphasizes the importance of artists; as an example of contrast, notice that according to imitation theory, art's function is to represent *the world*. Expression theory centers on the artist's inner life; one way to understand this is that, in an artwork, an artist offers her *affective reaction* to the world.

The expression theory has certainly been an influential theory; John Hospers, in his "The Concept of Artistic Expression" (1955)—which is critical of expression theory—begins by asserting, "The expression theory of art, in one form or another, has dominated the aesthetic scene for the past two centuries." Philosophers have also considered that works of art may be *expressive of* emotions—possessing expressive qualities—without being expressions of an artist's emotions. For more on this and other developments in expression theory, as well as more on Tolstoy's and Collingwood's views, see EMOTION, MUSIC.

Further Reading

Hospers, J. (1955), "The concept of artistic expression." *Proceedings of the Aristotelian Society*, 55: 313–44.

Ridley, A. (2005), "Expression in art," in J. Levinson (ed.), *The Oxford Handbook of Aesthetics*. Oxford and New York: Oxford University Press.

Tormey, A. (1971), *The Concept of Expression*. Princeton, NJ: Princeton University Press.

Feminist Critique

While feminist philosophers of art have contributed to philosophy of art on a range of issues, we will restrict ourselves here to a few central critiques feminists have launched against traditional philosophy of art. Some feminists hold that the very concept of art employed by philosophers is gendered. The various art forms became unified as the "fine arts" in the eighteenth century, grounded upon BEAUTY and the AESTHETIC, as well as imitation.

This categorization marginalizes the practical crafts, which were previously categorized with poetry, painting, and so on (viz., *technē*; see REPRESENTATION, the introduction, on the history of "fine art," and DEFINITION). Historically, a large portion of the creative work done by women was craftwork for domestic purposes; this eighteenth century re-categorization of art redefined women's creative work and removed many women from the history of art. (That women in past centuries engaged primarily in this sort of creative work—that is, that women, by and large, were not engaged in the fine arts—is explained by the fact that women were historically denied the requisite means and associations, the requisite economic and social conditions.)

Formalism emphasizes that works of art are autonomous, to be understood and evaluated based on their intrinsic properties. Like critical theorists (see ADORNO) and others (see DEWEY), many feminist philosophers of art believe that it is a mistake to examine art as cut off from life, detached from its context (see DISINTEREST). Feminists maintain that art's context is relevant both to understanding and evaluating art, where this context includes gender as well the social, political, historical, and so on. Relatedly, a number of philosophers in the tradition have maintained that there is a special attitude, a particular perceptual comportment, which it is proper or even required for spectators to adopt in relation to works of art; some feminist philosophers of art are critical of this traditional notion of DISINTEREST, the presupposition of a generic, ideal spectator. Such a perceptual perspective seems odd indeed; perhaps it is not even possible to adopt such a perspective that involves being active and passive—"actively finding the right psychical distance to let sensations be passively registered" (Hanson 2005, p. 563). Importantly, the tradition does not take note of the fact that this approach to art was conceived by persons of a certain race, social class, and gender—namely, white, upper-class males. Some feminist philosophers (and most continental philosophers) emphasize that persons situated differently experience art differently (for an emphasis on class differences, see Pierre BOURDIEU). This traditional approach not only limits the ways of engaging with art that are considered, and it not only prioritizes a privileged manner of engagement, but to return to our initial point, it devalues artistic work that is not typically engaged with in a disinterested manner, such as craftwork.

Further Reading

Brand, P. and Korsmeyer, C. (eds) (1995), *Feminism and Tradition in Aesthetics*. University Park: Pennsylvania State University Press.

Eaton, A. (2008), "Feminist philosophy of art," *Philosophy Compass*, 3(4).

Hanson, K. (2005), "Feminist aesthetics," in D. M. Lopes and B. Gaut (eds), *The Routledge Companion to Aesthetics* (2nd edn). New York: Routledge Press.

Korsmeyer, C. (2004), *Gender and Aesthetics*. New York and London: Routledge.

Formalism

Consider a few rough approximations before turning to particular formalist theories. A work of art's form consists of its perceptual components and their relations; emphasizing the latter results in taking a work's form to be its structure. Formalism states that a work of art's structure, form, design is the principal element in virtue of which it attains art status (see DEFINING ART), and is also the locus of the VALUE OF ART. Relatedly, a common way to draw the distinction between form and content is to characterize a work of art's form as the *way* in which the subject matter (the content) is presented or organized. The form of literature involves syntax, rhyme, and larger structural elements. The form of a painting consists of lines, shapes, colors, and their arrangement. The form of a film involves features such as camera angles, blocking, lighting. The form of dance involves body movements, orientation, and so on. The form of a musical work is what we find represented in a score: harmonic, melodic, and rhythmic relationships.

Although formalists direct us to these structural features of works of art, they do not merely emphasize that works of art possess some form or another (after all, a chair, an apartment, and a city have a form); rather, they maintain that works of art have a special sort of form. According to a formalist such as Clive BELL, what makes an artifact a work of art is this special sort of form; Bell calls art's form "significant form" (but note that Bell restricts his claims to visual art). Eduard Hanslick (1825–1904) calls the special form of the musical work of art "beautiful form." Another maneuver a formalist may make is to grant that some nonart objects possess significant form, such as a scientific hypothesis or a chair, but emphasize that these are not works of art because they primarily serve a function other than exhibiting their form; art's primary purpose is to display its form. In order to perceive a work of art's form, a perceiver cannot get caught up in the way in which the work of art speaks to practical or personal interests. Some notion of DISINTERESTED perception often accompanies formalism. If you are watching a horror film, for instance, becoming actually scared, or calling out to a character— "*look out!*"—this is to fail to perceive the form properly, as a result of being caught up in the representational and expressive content (see EMOTION). Approaching the relationship between disinterest and formalism from the other angle, if one holds that the proper way to perceive works of art is with disinterest, then one is likely to take art's core properties to be formal. Immanuel Kant's account of AESTHETIC JUDGMENT involves a formalist dimension, as well as an influential emphasis upon disinterest (see KANT, *CRITIQUE OF JUDGMENT*). Aristotle may be deemed a protoformalist, insofar as he understands plot to be the arrangement of events, and he takes plot to be the most important feature of tragedy (see ARISTOTLE, *POETICS*).

Formalists maintain that works of art are independent, autonomous. In emphasizing form, formalists are emphasizing intrinsic properties of works of art, not what works of art may express, arouse, or represent. In a REPRESENTATION theory or an EXPRESSION theory, art is defined and valued relationally, for how well works represent, how accurately they embody an artist's emotion, how well the work communicates an emotion to its spectators, and so on. According to formalism, works of art are not subservient to such functions. Nor is art understood in terms of whatever social, religious, or political functions it may perform.

Formalism has important implications for the relationships between art, politics, and morality. PLATO famously criticized imitative art that possess subject matter that can negatively affect the young. According to a formalist, such concerns should not influence one's appraisal of works of art *qua* art. Formalism cordons off a work of art from the moral and political realms (but see ADORNO). Clive Bell takes representational content to be *irrelevant* to understanding and evaluating visual works of art. Consider a notoriously troubling example. Leni Riefenstahl's Nazi propaganda film, *Triumph of the Will* (1934). If the film is as formally outstanding, as many suggest, then according to formalism, its immoral content should not prevent us from considering it to be a great work of art. According to formalism, we can judge both that it is a great work of art and also that it is immoral and politically deleterious, without the latter judgments affecting the former. In Charlie Chaplin's *The Great Dictator* (1940), he pokes fun at Nazism, effectively critiquing Hitler, anti-semitism, and so on. The film has positive moral and political qualities, but according to formalism, these qualities are not relevant to an evaluation of the film *qua* art. Examples such as this one seem to place strain on this formalist claim; part of the Chaplin film's value must lie in its cutting critique. Philosophers critical of Bell have argued that, even on a formalist view, representational content is far from irrelevant to art status and value (see the helpful discussion in Carroll 1999, and Isenberg 1988). (See ETHICS.)

Formalism's de-emphasis of representational elements has benefits. For example, formalism is able to accommodate art forms that a representational theory struggles to accommodate, such as abstract art, nonrepresentational dance, and instrumental music. In addition, formalism provides a way of understanding how it is that a person from one culture can understand and be moved by art from a different culture, even if cultural differences prevent her from understanding a work's representational content.

Consider some problems with an essentialist formalist approach like Bell's. Are there objects that are clearly not works of art but which do possess significant or beautiful form? If so, these serve as counter-examples to the view. Are there objects that are clearly works of art that do *not* possess significant or beautiful form? If so, they serve as additional counter-examples. Is bad art possible on a formalist view? If possessing significant form makes an artifact a work of art, and if that makes a work of art good, how can there be bad works? It seems that artifacts are either good works of art or not works of art at all. But of course, the more cutting criticism of Bell's formalism is that he does not offer a clear account of significant form (see BELL, ART).

Eduard Hanslick (1825–1904) put forward an enduringly influential formalism of music in his *On the Musically Beautiful* (1854). Hanslick's formalism is pitted primarily against theories that conceive of music in terms of its ability to arouse and/or represent the emotions. Hanslick argued that the focus of musical aesthetics should be on musical structure, form, with an emphasis on music's autonomy. According to Hanslick, the content of music is "tonally moving forms." Bell claims that we know when a work possesses significant form because it will have the effect of arousing the "aesthetic emotion"; Hanslick's formalism does not possess this subjective component of Bell's theory; there is no phenomenon corresponding to Bell's aesthetic emotion. Just as Bell takes representation to be irrelevant to the aesthetic quality of visual art, Hanslick takes emotions to be irrelevant to the "musically beautiful." Formalists about music will also disregard any suggested representational elements, including lyrics, program notes, et cetera. Other prominent formalists include Roger Fry (1866–1934), and the art critic, Clement Greenberg (1909–94).

Finally, notice that the pure formalist position denies that a work of art's features are even partially determined by contextual or historical factors. Contrast this with the centrality of context in theories such as Arthur DANTO'S, George DICKIE'S, and Kendall WALTON'S. The centrality of context—whether it is a matter of apprehending works of art correctly or a matter of grasping their value—is also emphasized in a number of continental theories; see, for example, MARXISM, BOURDIEU, HEGEL, HEIDEGGER.

Further Reading

Carroll, N. (1985), "Formalism and critical evaluation," in P. McCormick (ed.), *The Reasons of Art*. Ottawa: University of Ottawa Press.
—(1999), *Philosophy of Art: A Contemporary Introduction*. London and New York: Routledge Press.
Fry, R. (1956), *Vision and Design*. New York: Meridian.
Greenberg, C. (1961), *Art and Culture*. Boston: Beacon.
Hanslick, E. (1986 [1854]), *On the Musically Beautiful*, G. Payzant (trans.). Indianapolis: Hackett.
Isenberg, A. (1988), "Formalism," in W. Callaghan, L. Cauman, and C. G. Hempel (eds), *Aesthetics and the Theory of Criticism: Selected Essays of Arnold Isenberg*. Chicago and London: University Of Chicago Press.

Institutional Theory of Art, see Dickie, George

Interpretation

The general aim of interpretation is to deepen our appreciation of a work of art by improving our understanding of it. This involves identifying the important elements of a work and coming to understand how they contribute to its meaning and value. This may involve making sense of the conceptual and expressive meaning of a literary work, making sense of the representational content of a visual work, making sense of the structural relations of a work of instrumental music, and so on. But what is relevant to interpreting a work of art? Initially, it seems obvious that we should seek out the artist's view of the work—what meaning did she intend the work to convey? On this traditional, intentionalist view, an interpretation is to be grounded on the artist's intentions; the artist's will determines a work's meaning; the intended meaning just is the meaning of the work of art. The interpreter, then, should strive to uncover what the artist meant to convey. This is a reasonable view, if works of art are sufficiently similar to statements asserted in a conversation: in the attempt to understand an interlocutor's meaning, we try to discover what he intended. (An intentionalist view is put forward in E. D. Hirsch's *Validity in Interpretation*.)

Anti-intentionalists believe that artists' intentions are irrelevant to interpreting their work; interpretation should focus on works of art themselves. W. K. Wimsatt and Monroe BEARDSLEY suggest that if a writer's intended meaning is not successfully realized in a work of art, then her intentions are not instructive in uncovering the meaning in the work; if her intended meaning is realized in the work, then we can disregard those intentions and simply focus on the work. This anti-intentionalism lent support to New Criticism. Structuralists also argue against intentionalism, claiming that a literary text's meaning rests, not on the will of the author, but on the underlying, public structures of the language, structures determining grammar and meaning.

In a further worry about intentionalism, notice that an artist's intentions occasionally misfire; an artist may intend to create a work with one meaning but end up imputing it with another. In such a case, interpreting a work guided by the artist's intentions would lead to an incorrect interpretation. There are interesting cases in which an artist accomplishes something *more* profound than he or she set out to accomplish. An unusual example may be the rock and roll guitarist and songwriter Chuck Berry (b. 1926). Judging from comments in his autobiography, and interviews in the film, *Hail! Hail! Rock and Roll* (1987), Berry seems to have intended primarily to write songs that would sell, by writing about themes popular with teenagers, such as cars, love, school, and so on. If it is reasonable to take this to be his pervasive intention, he accomplished much more than he intended. Although an overstatement, John Lennon remarked that Berry is, "the greatest rock and roll poet" (interview in aforementioned film).

Although continental philosophers such as Roland BARTHES (1915–80), Michel Foucault, and Jacques Derrida agree that the meaning of a work is not determined by an author, they go further than Wimsatt and Beardsley in maintaining that there is not one, determinate meaning of a work; consequently, it cannot be the goal of interpretation to discover that one meaning. These poststructuralists reason that once we discard the author as a fixer of the work's meaning, then there is no sense to supposing that there is only one meaning. The underlying structure that grounds meaning does not fix one meaning; there is an openness allowing for multiple interpretations of a text. Barthes draws a distinction between a "work" and a "text"; the meaning of a text is open. A text is produced by the activity of a reader. The reader, like an author, creates meaning. Barthes distinguishes between "readerly," interpretations of a text (where the reader is passive), and "writerly" interpretations (where the reader is active and creative). Authors of writerly texts look upon the reader's interpretation as a part of the work.

A view explored by a number of philosophers in the last several years is *hypothetical intentionalism*. This view states that intentions are, indeed, relevant to a work's meaning, but the intentions at issue may not be the actual intentions of the artist but rather hypothesized intentions. Perhaps the intentions are those most justifiably attributed to an author of the work, given the work's features, and so on (see Jerrold Levinson 1996).

Above, it was noted that interpretation occasionally involves making sense of the structural relations of a work of instrumental music. Musicians play a role in this interpretive task, since through their choices they can encourage listeners to hear certain relations over others. One way in which musicians accomplish this is by means of minute variations of pitch and timing, known as expressive variations or musical nuances. These variations are often conceived as ways of leading a listener to hear a piece's structure in one way rather than another. Similarly, dancers interpret choreographed works, and actors interpret scripts. Regarding such performative interpretations, the *open* nature of interpretation seems to be emphasized. Musicians and actors, for example, are often lauded for novel interpretations.

Conceptual art raises interesting interpretive issues. The principal feature of conceptual art is the idea, conception, or meaning. Conceptual artists de-emphasize the perceivable object, the physical medium, in favor of the idea. In fact, the ideas that anchor conceptual works are often imperceptible; conceptual works of art can be perceptually indistinguishable from ordinary objects (consider Andy Warhol's *Brillo Box*; see Danto). Consequently, interpreting conceptual art seems to require considering, and in fact, prioritizing the intentions of artists. A conceptual work of art's perceivable properties will often get us nowhere. Regarding such works, we may not be able to determine that they are even works of art without considering the intentions of artists.

Further Reading

Berry, Chuck (1989), *Chuck Berry: The Autobiography*. Harmony Books. (See p. 139.)
Hackford, Taylor (director) (1987), *Hail! Hail Rock and Roll*. Delilah Films.
Hirsch, E. D. (1967), *Validity in Interpretation*. New Haven: Yale University Press.
Levinson, J. (1996), *The Pleasures of Aesthetics*. Ithaca, NY: Cornell University Press.
Lyas, Colin (1997), *Aesthetics*. London: University College London Press.
Stecker, R. (1996), *Art Works: Definition, Meaning, Value*. University Park: Pennsylvania State University.
Wimsatt, W. K. and Beardsley, M. C. (1946), "The intentional fallacy," *Sewanee Review*, 54: 468–88.

Marxism

G. W. F. Hegel held that *Geist* (spirit, mind) drives history forward. History does not proceed arbitrarily; it unfolds rationally, aiming toward a goal (the goal is individual human freedom). Karl Marx (incorrectly, it so happens) takes Hegel to mean that mere *ideas* move history forward. Thus, Marx takes his own view of the progress of history—as grounded in systems of economic production—to be an inversion of Hegel's view. Marx holds that material conditions move history forward, not ideas.

Marx conceives of these material conditions in terms of a society's *substructure*, the forces and social relations of economic production. These vary in different societies: the substructure of a primitive hunting society, for example, is different from the substructure of feudalism, and both are different from the substructure of capitalism, which is the focus of a Marxist critique. A society's *superstructure* consists of its ideology: its philosophy, religion, political theory, art, and so on. The traditional view of the relationship between ideology and material conditions (consider Marx's misinterpretation of Hegel above) is that ideology is more or less autonomous, and ideology has an historical influence upon material conditions.

In one sense or another, Marxists believe that a society's substructure affects its superstructure. Does the substructure cause, determine, condition, limit, or influence the superstructure? Under capitalism, the material conditions involve a class of capitalists, who own the means of production, and a class of exploited workers. If the relation between the substructure and superstructure is a strict one in which the substructure causes or determines the superstructure, then the works of art of a society may be simply a reflection of the substructure—as Marx and Engels write, in "The German Ideology," a "direct efflux" (1978, p. 154). But Marx's view shifted, and he did not take the relationship between art and a society's substructure to be so clear cut (see Marx's discussion of Greek art in "The Grundrisse.")

A Marxist theorist will want to carve out free space in this connection between substructure and superstructure in order for art to engage in some sort of effective critique of capitalism—that will be the locus of the VALUE OF ART. One approach is Georg Lukács's (1885–1971), who maintains that art can provide a more vivid and more accurate depiction of society than any other means of knowing (relatedly, he lauded realism in literature). The thought is that such a vivid depiction would awaken the working classes to their actual circumstances.

Marxists believe that the ideology of a society is controlled, in one sense or another, by the dominant class, and moreover, that the ideology furthers the interests of that class. This has led some

Marxists to believe (Adorno, for example) that the art under capitalism typically reinforces the sociopolitical status quo. Art that is mere entertainment, for instance, serves as a palliative, only temporarily relieving the suffering of the exploited class. THEODOR W. ADORNO did not see the role of art as Lukács did. Rather, he endorses art that is free of representational content; abstract art and instrumental music model freedom through their autonomy. Adorno praises, in particular, avant-garde art, especially atonal music, for its intellectually challenging nature—and that's the key—the challenge fosters a listener's independent thinking and critical disposition, predisposing her to be socially and politically critical.

Critics of Marxism maintain that it is ultimately reductive; Marxism illegitimately reduces aesthetic judgment, for example, to nothing but a mere preference of those in a particular social class. See POLITICS; POPULAR ART; VALUE OF ART; FILM; PHOTOGRAPHY; BENJAMIN; BOURDIEU; HEGEL, *LECTURES ON FINE ART*.

Further Reading

Eagleton, T. (1990), *The Ideology of the Aesthetic*. Oxford: Blackwell.
Marcuse, H. (1979), *The Aesthetic Dimension: Toward A Critique of Marxist Aesthetics*. Boston: Beacon Press.
Marx, K. and Engels, F. (1978), *The Marx-Engels Reader* (2nd edn). R. C. Tucker (ed.), W. W. Norton & Company. See especially "The German ideology: part I," 146–200, and "The Grundrisse," 221–93.
Munro, T. (1960), "The Marxist theory of art history: socio-economic determinism and the dialectical process." *The Journal of Aesthetics and Art Criticism*, 18(4): 430–45.
Wood, A. W. (1993), "Hegel and Marxism," in F. C. Beiser (ed.), *The Cambridge Companion to Hegel*. Cambridge: Cambridge University Press.

Metaphor

A metaphor is a figurative use of language, which, according to a traditional account, turns on a *comparison* between two very different things; for example, "Man is a wolf"; "Juliet is the sun." In one sense or another, the first term is likened to the second, and the comparison encourages us to think differently about the first. Making sense of metaphors is obviously required for INTERPRETATIONS and evaluations of literature.

ARISTOTLE suggests that metaphors are closely related to similes. A subsequent tradition explicitly takes metaphors to be similes; "Time is a river" is identical to "Time is like a river." On this view, metaphors are reducible to literal statements. But stating that X is *like* Y (a simile) is different from stating that X *is* Y (a metaphor). Saying that time is *like* a river is different from saying that time *is* a river. The former is literally true; the latter, literally false. Thus, it seems that metaphors are not identical to similes. (However, some philosophers—Ted Cohen, for example—deny that such a simile is literal.)

Beginning with the influential essay, "Metaphor" (1954), Max Black proposes what he calls an "interaction" theory of metaphor. He maintains that metaphors *create* similarities rather than present known similarities. And he emphasizes that metaphors cannot be paraphrased in literal language. In the metaphor, "Man is a wolf," "man" is the principal subject; "wolf" is the subsidiary subject. Through the interactions of commonplace beliefs associated with each subject, *some* of the ideas associated with the subsidiary subject are related to the principal subject; determining which are related requires a consideration of the context (man is not furry, does not walk on four legs, but he can be vicious). Nelson GOODMAN develops an account of metaphor that is related to Black's; metaphor is at the center of Goodman's theory of EXPRESSION. He suggests that works of art that are believed to express sadness (say) *metaphorically exemplify* sadness.

For NIETZSCHE, metaphor is not a mere rhetorical device. In his controversial "On Truth and Lie in an Extra-Moral Sense" (1873), he challenges the traditional correspondence theory of truth; truth, he asserts, is not a matter of certain representations or concepts that track reality; rather, perception and knowledge are metaphorical at the core. Ordinary perception and understanding are similar to artistic CREATIVITY and INTERPRETATION. The more stable truths of a culture are simply dead metaphors.

Further Reading

Black, M. (1955), "Metaphor." *Proceedings of the Aristotelian Society*, 55: 273–94.

Cohen, T. (1975), "Figurative speech and figurative acts." *Journal of Philosophy*, 72: 669–84.

Davidson, D. (1978). "What metaphors mean." *Critical Inquiry*, 5: 31–47.

Nietzsche, F. (1994), "On truth and lie in an extra-moral sense," in D. Breazeale (ed.), *Philosophy and Truth: Selections from Nietzsche's Notebooks of the Early 1870s.* Atlantic Highlands: Humanities Press, pp. 79–91.

Nature

It is a common observation that we can have AESTHETIC EXPERIENCES of nature—a waterfall, an ocean view, a bird song, and so on. Eighteenth-century philosophers such as Francis Hutcheson and Immanuel KANT viewed natural objects as primary examples of BEAUTY and the AESTHETIC. Traditionally, the notion of DISINTERESTED contemplation is key. We appreciate the beauty in nature by detaching or distancing ourselves from our personal and practical interests. Regarding the SUBLIME, instead of being terrified in the face of powerful natural phenomena, such as hurricanes and tornados, from a place of safety at least, we can appreciate nature's power aesthetically by means of this kind of perceptual detachment. Late eighteenth-century theorists suggested an additional aesthetic category, situated *between* the beautiful and the sublime—the *picturesque*. More complex and less uniform than the beautiful; forceful, but not as powerful as the sublime. Approaching nature in this picture-like manner means to focus on the qualities in a natural scene that we might focus on in a landscape painting.

Beginning with G. W. F. HEGEL's (1770–1831) view, art was emphasized over nature. Subsequently, the meaning of "aesthetics" shifted toward denoting the philosophy of art; concern for the aesthetics of nature dissipated. In the second half of twentieth century, interest returned largely through R. W. Hepburn's influential "Contemporary Aesthetics and the Neglect of Natural Beauty" (1966). This relatively new subfield of the philosophy of art is known as *environmental aesthetics*. Hepburn draws interesting distinctions between aesthetic experiences of art and aesthetic experiences of nature. Consider two: First, he points out that works of art are set apart from their environments by being *framed* (he means to include in this concept devices employed by other art forms as well, such as taking place on a stage); natural objects are frameless, unbounded. Second, aesthetic experiences of nature are not disinterested or detached, whereas that perceptual perspective features prominently in the traditional view of aesthetic experiences of art. Hepburn observes that in aesthetic experiences of nature we are not separated from the situation; rather, we are *involved* with it, sometimes enveloped by it. Arnold Berleant develops this approach, and puts forward an aesthetics of nature centered on active engagement rather than disinterested contemplation. Perceiving nature aesthetically requires perceptually immersing ourselves in it.

Allen Carlson draws upon theories of art that highlight the importance of a work of art's historical context for adequate understanding and evaluation (see ONTOLOGY; VALUE OF ART; DANTO; WALTON). He claims that an accurate understanding and aesthetic evaluation of nature requires knowledge about the natural object(s) at issue, that is, relevant information from the natural sciences. Carlson's may be regarded as a cognitivist view, and perhaps Berleant's view can be regarded as noncognitivist, insofar as it emphasizes perceptual immersion.

Further Reading

Berleant, A. (1991), *Art and Engagement*. Philadelphia: Temple University Press.
Berleant, A. and Carlson, A. (eds) (1998), *Special Issue: Environmental Aesthetics, Journal of Aesthetics and Art Criticism*, 56.
Budd, M. (2002), *The Aesthetic Appreciation of Nature*. Oxford: Oxford University Press.
Carlson, A. (1981), "Nature, aesthetic judgment, and objectivity," *Journal of Aesthetics and Art Criticism*, 40: 15–27.
Hepburn, R. (1966), "Contemporary aesthetics and the neglect of natural beauty," in B. Williams and A. Montefiori (eds), *British Analytical Philosophy*. London: Routledge & Kegan Paul, pp. 285–310.

Ontology

Ontology is the study of *being*, in the most basic sense. Inquiring into the ontology of works of art is to wonder about what kind of thing a work of art is, what kind of entity. Are works of art physical things like hula hoops? Are works of art mental entities like ideas? Are works of art abstract objects like the number seven? Perhaps paintings are one kind of thing (say, physical objects) and musical works are another kind of thing (say, abstract structures). That is, perhaps there is no one kind of entity that all works of art are; perhaps works of art are two, three, or many different kinds of thing. Perhaps works of art are events; Gregory Currie has argued that works of art—all works of art—are events, action-types.

Regarding the relationship between DEFINING ART and the ontology of art, getting art's ontological status right will not yield a definition of art. Even if all works of art turn out to be the same kind of thing (say, physical things), it will not be a kind of thing that only works of art are (hula hoops and mountains are also physical things, obviously). Ontology is relevant, however, to describing, interpreting, and evaluating works of art, since different ontological positions will result in attributing different properties to works of art.

It may seem reasonable to hold that paintings and sculptures are physical objects. But notice that a painting, the work of art, is not identical to a painted canvas. There is a certain amount of imaginative work a perceiver must do in order to perceive a painted work of art. For example, where a painting has a dark, thick line, we may imaginatively perceive a shadow; where a painting has a certain oval shape, we may imaginatively perceive a man's head. This shadow and the head are not there in the physical object, but they may considered to be a part of the work of art imaginatively perceived.

Such considerations led R. G. COLLINGWOOD to adopt an idealist ontology of art, in his *PRINCIPLES OF ART*. He maintains that a painting, for instance, is not to be identified with the painted canvas; a painting is a mental object. (The phenomenologist Edmund Husserl and the existential phenomenologist Jean-Paul Sartre held related views.) A poem or a tune may exist even though it has never been written, spoken, or hummed; it exists in the artist's head. This mental object is the creative product, the work of art. More accurately, Collingwood maintains that the work of art is not a thing, but an activity. The work of art is the "total imaginative experience." According to his view, the publicly available object (the painted canvas, the sounds, the written poem) provides a way for the spectator to reconstruct the work of art in her own mind. In other words, when I look at Van

Gogh's *The Bridge at Trinquetaille* (1888), I am not looking at the actual work of art; rather, I use that painted canvas to reconstruct in imagination the work of art, which is an idea in the artist's mind. Consider a few counterintuitive implications of this view; if works of art are mental entities or activities, the work of art will cease to exist once the artist has finished creating it, or at least, when she stops thinking about it. Also, if we take the work to exist only in the minds of spectators, then each work of art, each *Mona Lisa*, each *Hamlet*, will be different. The idealist ontology also seems to undervalue the work of art's medium; paint, canvas, sounds in music, and actual body movement in dance seem too important to devalue as the idealist does.

Returning to the physical ontology, this ontological view seems hard to swallow in relation to art forms such as music, literature, film, and so on. What kind of physical thing might Tolstoy's *Anna Karenina* be? Notice that it is not the original manuscript; in cases where the original manuscript is destroyed, we do not believe that the work of art ceases to exist as well. Although a particular performance of Beethoven's Fifth Symphony may be characterized as a physical event, consisting of a particular collection of sounds, Beethoven's Fifth Symphony does not cease to exist once a given performance is finished, and it does not spring back into existence when the next performance begins.

This train of thought leads to the realization that some kinds of artworks are *singular* (paintings, frescos, noncast sculptures, and so on) and others are *multiple* (music, literature, plays, photographs, and cast sculptures). While the *Mona Lisa* exists only in one place at one time, Beethoven's Fifth Symphony may be performed in multiple locations simultaneously. Nelson GOODMAN draws a similar distinction between *autographic* and *allographic* art forms. Painting, sculpture, and etchings are examples of autographic art forms; music, literature, theatre, and dance are examples of allographic art forms (architecture is a mixed art form). Notation is at the core of this distinction; autographic art forms do not admit of notation; allographic art forms do. Also, the distinction between an original and a forgery is important regarding autographic works, whereas it is not regarding allographic works. As long as my copy of *Moby Dick* contains the same words and so on, as the original, then it is an instance of *Moby Dick*. As long as a performance of Ravel's *Bolero* complies with the score (with the notation), then it is a performance of that work (note, however, that Goodman's claim here is counterintuitive: one small mistake in a performance of *Bolero* means that it fails to be a performance of that work.) Books and performances that do not comply in these ways are not forgeries; they are simply not instances of the given works. The identity of an autographic work depends upon its history of production; a forgery has a different history of production. But note that this distinction is not identical to the distinction between singular and multiple works of art. Although all singular works of art are autographic, some multiple works are also autographic; etchings and woodcuts, for example, are autographic but multiple.

What kind of entity is a work of music or literature? Drawing from the work of the pragmatist Charles Sanders Peirce, Richard WOLLHEIM (and others) have construed multiple works as *types*, and their instances (performances or copies) as *tokens*. Consider a question we just brushed by above, in relation to Goodman—what makes a token a token of a given work? Consider music—what makes a performance a performance of Beethoven's *Fifth*? One common answer is that the performance has a certain musical structure, which is represented in a score of the *Fifth*. (We have just seen Goodman's strict version of this compliance view above.) Thus, when we ask the question—what sort of type is a musical work?—we might say that a musical work is a kind of abstract structure, a pattern of sounds. A simple example of an abstract structure is a square; just as many squares can be drawn, many instances of a given work of music can be performed. Similarly, perhaps a photograph is a certain visual structure; a literary work is a certain linguistic structure. Two serious problems with the structural ontology are that, first, it entails that works of art are no more created than the number seven; they are merely discovered or selected. This seems counterintuitive. In addition, on this view, works of art cannot be destroyed. An ontology that requires us to adopt the position that works of art are not created, seems too dissonant with our pretheoretical understanding of art (Jerrold Levinson has stressed this in his "What a Musical Work Is" [1980]). It is important to note Goodman's divergence from such views, which rests on his nominalism. A nominalist maintains that abstract objects do not exist; thus, according to Goodman, the musical work (say) is not an abstract structure (and it is also not the score); rather, the musical work is the set of performances that comply with the score.

A family of related views that aim to overcome the shortcomings of those above can be called contextualist; according to such a view, a part of what fixes a work of art's identity and content are aspects of its art-historical context. A token is a token of a given work of art in virtue of not only its properties that are intrinsic to the token but extrinsic properties as well. Two works of art (singular or multiple works) may be perceptually identical and structurally identical, yet be different works that possess different aesthetic properties, content, and value, due to contextual factors. For example, Jerrold Levinson argues that musical works are *created* abstract objects ("initiated types") but their structural features are not their only features: the musico-historical context and instrumentation specifications are also features of a work of music (see his "What a Musical Work Is," in his 1990). See PHENOMENOLOGY, DANTO, WALTON.

Further Reading

Currie, Gregory (1989), *An Ontology of Art*. London: Macmillan.
Ingarden, R. (1989 [1962]), *The Ontology of the Work of Art*, R. Meyer with J. T. Goldthwait (trans.). Athens, OH: Ohio University Press.
Levinson, J. (1990), *Music, Art and Metaphysics: Essays in Philosophical Aesthetics*. Ithaca, NY: Cornell University Press.
Thomasson, A. (2004), "The ontology of art," in P. Kivy (ed.), *The Blackwell Guide to Aesthetics*. Oxford: Wiley-Blackwell.
Wolterstorff, N. (1980), *Works and Worlds of Art*. Oxford: Clarendon Press.

Phenomenology

A wide range of philosophers who have very different views are considered phenomenologists: Edmund Husserl (1859–1938), Martin HEIDEGGER (1889–1976), Roman Ingarden (1893–1970), Jean-Paul Sartre (1905–80), Maurice Merleau-Ponty (1908–61), Mikel Dufrenne (1910–95), among others. Phenomenology has more to do with how one does philosophy than with a particular doctrine or set of doctrines. In fact, roughly speaking, the phenomenological method rests on attempting to attend to an object one sets out to examine in a way that is as free as possible from theoretical assumptions and beliefs. Existential phenomenologists (such as Heidegger and Merleau-Ponty) begin by carefully describing how things show up in such pretheoretical experiences, "lived" experiences, whether they are investigating human being, free will, the body, or works of art. Their subsequent claims are typically supported with reference to those pretheoretical experiences.

Scattered about in his *Phenomenology of Perception* (1945), and featured in his "Cézanne's Doubt" (1945), is Merleau-Ponty's suggestion that certain painters, like phenomenologists, elucidate lived-experience. A number of Cézanne's paintings from the late nineteenth century include oddly swollen saucers, warped and extended tables, out of kilter baseboards, and so on. What some of Cezanne's critics derisively referred to as distortions, Merleau-Ponty understood to be indications that Cézanne was depicting phenomena as we experience them pretheoretically. Cézanne was attempting to paint as we see; what is more, he was endeavoring to paint the very process of objects emerging in perception. Cézanne was not painting what he *should* see (in light of a vision theory or according to geometric perspective); rather, he was painting what he actually saw.

We can observe a number of the maneuvers a phenomenologist might make in an examination of art by considering the work of one of Husserl's students, Roman Ingarden. In his *The Literary Work of Art*, Ingarden maintains that the literary work of art (LWA) is an intentional object. Phenomenologists use the term "intentional" in a special way; for the phenomenologist, "to intend" is not to do something on purpose; rather, "to intend" is to be mentally directed toward something (mentally directed in a perception, a thought, et cetera). An intentional object, then, is the object of such an intention; for example, if I think *about* Jill Rosenberg, then she is the intentional object of my thought; I may also think *about* a vampire with a soul, in which case a vampire with a soul, a nonexistent thing, is the intentional object.

By defining the LWA as an intentional object, Ingarden was aiming to overcome the ONTOLOGICAL problems that arise in taking works of art to be ideal or physical objects. Ingarden's LWA is mind-dependent but not a mere imaginary object; it transcends particular intentional acts. The LWA is a "stratified formation," consisting of both real and ideal components, which form an organic whole. Roughly speaking, the strata, the layers, are word sounds, units of meaning, schematized aspects, and represented objects. The schematized aspects are the many aspects of the subject matter that are left incomplete, indeterminate, which the reader fleshes out in her reading experience. The reader's work of fleshing out this and other aspects of the LWA, is what Ingarden calls "concretizing." The LWA (the *artistic* object) is to be distinguished from the *aesthetic* object; the latter is the intentional object that results from concretizing reading experiences; the LWA, then, is a potential aesthetic object. Ingarden's view is quite fecund regarding evaluation, since each layer of the LWA can be evaluated, as well as various interrelations among the layers, in terms of *artistic* value, while *aesthetic* value can be considered with respect to the aesthetic object.

Heidegger believed that describing things as they show up in pretheoretical experience means giving an account of why we make sense of things as we do. He explored the bases of intelligibility, which he calls *being* (on one interpretation). Heidegger believed that the best works of art can create new cultural paradigms; they can open up a "world" that grounds new ways of understanding things, events, and people. For example, he claims that a Greek temple *gathers* the world of Greek culture and religion; it *unifies* what many things and events mean for that culture. See HEIDEGGER, "THE ORIGIN OF THE WORK OF ART"; DEWEY.

Further Reading

Dufrenne, M. (1973), *The Phenomenology of Aesthetic Experience*, E. Casey (trans.). Evanston, IL: Northwestern University Press.
Ingarden, R. (1973a), *The Literary Work of Art*, G. G. Grabowicz (trans.). Evanston, IL: Northwestern University Press.
—(1973b), *The Cognition of the Literary Work of Art*, R. A. Crowley and K. R. Olsen (trans.). Evanston, IL: Northwestern University Press.
Johnson, G. A. (ed.) (1993), *The Merleau-Ponty Aesthetics Reader: Philosophy and Painting*, M. B. Smith (trans. & ed.). Evanston, IL: Northwestern University Press.
Merleau-Ponty, M. (2012 [1945]), *Phenomenology of Perception*, D. Landes (trans.). London and New York: Routledge.
Moran, D. (2013), *Introduction to Phenomenology* (2nd edn). London: Routledge.
Sartre, J. P. (1988), *"What Is Literature?" and Other Essays*. Cambridge, MA: Harvard University Press.

Politics

"Musical modes are never changed without a change in the most important of a city's laws." This is a quotation from PLATO'S *REPUBLIC*, written in approximately 360 B.C.E. (book IV). Philosophy's preoccupation with the relationship between art and politics goes back. But what is Plato getting at? Plato believed that a person's soul must be in balance in order for that person to recognize justice and to act accordingly. The wrong kinds of art can prevent a young person's soul from attaining the proper balance, and, it can throw a soul out of balance. The final piece of the puzzle is simpler: whichever laws are put in place by the individuals that constitute a society will depend upon their conceptions of justice. Art affects minds, and people make laws. Plato took this critique quite far by maintaining that, in an ideal state, most kinds of art will be prohibited (see CENSORSHIP, ETHICS).

Art can be very effective in *supporting* one political ideology or another. Presidential candidates in the United States, for example, often use very specific popular music at rallies, for commercials, and so on. In addition, candidates invite famous actors and musicians to make personal appearances on their behalf. Of course, the content of art can also promote a political agenda; consider Leni Reifenstahl's innovative, beautiful and troubling Nazi propaganda film, *Triumph of the Will* (1934).

More subtly, following a MARXIST train of thought, Theodor W. ADORNO argues that art which is merely pleasing, entertaining—rather than intellectually and aesthetically challenging—functions as a palliative, temporarily relieving the suffering of the exploited but not stirring them to face up to their exploitation. Ultimately, such art dulls spectators' critical inclinations, fostering both artistic and political conformism, reinforcing the status quo. Adorno conceives of POPULAR ART, such as popular music and Hollywood films, as functioning in this way. When asked for his opinion about the Vietnam War, the singer Elvis Presley had a standard answer; a portion of it was to remark, "I'm just an entertainer" (Hampton 2008, p. 156). According to Adorno's view, this does not establish the political neutrality of the singer or his music.

Art can also *oppose* a political ideology or candidate by means of its content. For example, a number of Israeli artists create work that challenges the Israeli political right by sympathetically depicting the

Palestinian struggle. More generally, consider protest art, subversive art, and so on. Another way in which some Marxists believe that art can be politically effective is by merely showing unjust aspects of a society's material conditions in order to raise awareness. In contrast to Adorno, Walter BENJAMIN holds that the popular arts, such as jazz music and Hollywood films, constitute a break with tradition that leads to new ways of experiencing art and new political forms of art.

But this explicit, content-based manner is not the only way that art can oppose an ideology. Again, Adorno's view is more subtle. He maintains that art that opposes an ideology explicitly via its content is *less* politically effective than abstract art and instrumental music, which models freedom through its autonomy. This is quite paradoxical, since one would expect that once art dispenses with its means of conceptual representation, it would cease to have political efficacy. How do such works of art function politically, in addition to simply modeling freedom? Adorno praises, in particular, avant-garde art, especially atonal music, for its intellectually challenging nature—and that's the key—which fosters in audiences independent thinking and a critical disposition, predisposing them to be socially and politically critical.

Pierre BOURDIEU traces a relationship between art and politics in terms of the very understanding of art that the philosophical tradition has developed. He takes the predominant view of art to be that works of art are autonomous objects that can only be recognized as such through DISINTERESTED perception, emphasizing form over content (this is Bourdieu's interpretation of Immanuel KANT). The aptitude for engaging with art in this way is *taste*. Bourdieu sees this view as a mere description of how those in Kant's elite social class approached and understood art, which Kant then presented as a universal, objective philosophy of art and AESTHETIC JUDGMENT. Taste, which the working class lacks, serves as a mark of distinction. It is possible to determine which class a person belongs to by determining which kinds of art she prefers. Moreover, preferences in art *justify* one's class status, given that taste is required to appreciate the finer things in life (fine furniture, fine food, haute couture, and so on). If a person does not have taste, then there is justification for her not having access to the finer things in life. It is in this sense that taste can function as a tool of political domination. See FILM and PHOTOGRAPHY.

Further Reading

Goehr, L. (2005), "Art and politics," in J. Levinson (ed.), *The Oxford Handbook of Aesthetics*. Oxford and New York: Oxford University Press.

Hampton, W. (2008), *Elvis Presley*. New York: Penguin.

Popular Art

Since the late nineteenth century, a distinction has often been drawn between fine art (high art) and popular art (low art, mass art). Examples of fine art are opera, painting, and poetry; the popular arts include popular jazz and rock music, Hollywood films, and pulp fiction. Commonly, when the distinction is invoked, high art is taken to be more valuable than popular art; some claim that popular art is not art at all. Although the terms "mass art," "popular art," and "low art" are occasionally used interchangeably, they have different meanings. "Low art" is a term used disparagingly in contrast to high art; mass art is mass produced and/or mass consumed; popular art is either popular or aimed at popular consumption.

If the VALUE OF ART is due entirely to the pleasure it provides in experience (which is obviously disputable), and if there is only one kind of pleasure (which is also disputable), then it may be difficult to argue that high art is more pleasurable than low art. How might popular art be distinguished from fine art? Philosophers have made the following suggestions. Perhaps popular art is not as enduringly valued as fine art; that is, popular art does not stand the test of time. Perhaps popular art is less complex than fine art, contains fewer ambiguous elements, is more easily accessible, requires less effort—on such grounds, some philosophers argue that popular art appeals to persons with undeveloped and unsophisticated taste. David Hume, for instance, holds that popular (vulgar) taste is more idiosyncratic and changeable than refined taste (see HUME, "OF THE STANDARD OF TASTE").

If popular art can be digested by means of passive experience, if it is mere entertainment, then it will likely not require or activate INTERPRETATION, imagination, or an *active* AESTHETIC EXPERIENCE (see PHENOMENOLOGY). These may be reasons to doubt its art status (see DEFINING ART). More recently, however, philosophers have argued that popular art can be more complex than traditionally presumed; some popular works of art demand active engagement, focused attention, background knowledge, and interpretation. Consider the subtleties of guitar timbre in rock music or the subtleties of rhythm (groove) in jazz, hip-hop, and rock. Apprehending such subtleties is not a passive endeavor; it requires a familiarity with the musical tradition and detail-oriented attention.

Theodor W. ADORNO argues that since popular art is a commodity, it *must* be easily accessible; it cannot be perceptually and intellectually demanding; the audience of popular art *demands* the familiar. This is a political issue for Adorno; popular art dulls one's critical abilities and functions as a palliative. Popular art fosters political conformism; it is not ideologically neutral. Adorno lauds avant-garde art that is difficult and challenging to grasp; such art encourages independent thinking, hones our critical abilities, and cultivates the predisposition to be socially and politically critical. In contrast, Walter BENJAMIN sees in mass art a liberating potential.

Pierre BOURDIEU'S account of the dominant philosophy of art rests on his interpretation of Immanuel KANT; he emphasizes FORMALISM and DISINTEREST. Bourdieu maintains that the notion of taste at play here is a mere creation of culture; Kant took what was the upper class manner of dealing with art to be universal. Even though Bourdieu deflates Kant's view, he contends that the working-class preferences for certain music, films, novels, and so on—the working-class "aesthetic"—is not an actual aesthetic; it is defined only negatively in contrast to the bourgeois aesthetic. The problem rests on the emphasis on content in popular art at the expense of attention to form. Bourdieu has since been criticized (by Theodore Gracyk and Richard Shusterman, for example), both for misunderstanding popular art and for misunderstanding Kant. See FILM, MUSIC, PHOTOGRAPHY and DEWEY.

Further Reading

Benjamin, W. (1969), "The work of art in the age of mechanical reproduction," *Illuminations*, H. Zohn (trans.). New York: Shocken.
Carroll, N. (1998), *A Philosophy of Mass Art*. Oxford: Oxford University Press.
Cohen, T. (1993), "High and low thinking about High and low art." *Journal of Aesthetics and Art Criticism*, 51: 151–6.

Gracyk, T. (2007), *Listening to Popular Music: Or, How I Learned to Stop Worrying and Love Led Zeppelin*. Ann Arbor: The University of Michigan Press.

Greenberg, C. (1939), "Avant-garde and kitsch," in J. O'Brien (ed.), *Clement Greenberg: The Collected Essays and Criticism* (vol. 1). Chicago: University of Chicago Press, 1986, pp. 5–22.

Shusterman, R. (2000), *Pragmatist Aesthetics: Living Beauty, Rethinking Art*. Lanham: Rowman & Littlefield.

Representation

PLATO maintains that painters and poets represent their subject matter by imitating it, copying; actors in a tragedy, for instance, represent individuals by copying their actions. On the imitation view, pictorial representation, depiction, rests on resemblance. A painting of a horse depicts a horse because it looks like a horse. (The Greek word that is translated with "representation," or "imitation," is "*mimēsis*.") This account of art endured. Although Plato was not suggesting a theory of all the fine arts—he could not, of course, because the Greeks grouped the arts and other practices differently than we do—the imitation approach still dominated at the point of the unification of the fine arts in the eighteenth century. Charles Batteux, in 1747, defines art as "the imitation of beautiful nature" (see the introduction, DEFINING ART, and BEAUTY). If, today, we consider the imitation theory as a definition of art, it fails. Imitation is not a necessary condition of art: there are clear examples of works of art that are not imitative (consider instrumental music and abstract painting). Moreover, imitation is not a sufficient condition of art: there are imitations that are not art (consider children imitating mermaids in a game).

Philosophers began to find fault with the imitation theory not only as a means of defining art but also as an account of artistic representation; they began to consider other ways of explaining how it is that works of art represent their subject matter. For the remainder of this entry, we will briefly consider what philosophers have had to say about pictorial representation, a.k.a depiction, which is the kind of representation one finds in painting, photography, cinematography, and so on (of the visual arts, sculpture is not pictorial).

According to the art historian Ernst Gombrich (1909–2001), artists do not passively copy what they see; there is no "innocent eye." Rather, seeing is a kind of interpretation influenced by pictorial conventions, such as the rules of perspective, and cultural conventions, as well as a painter's individual characteristics. Pictorial representation is not a matter of resemblance but of using conventional signs ("schemas") to stand for things. A circle does not represent a face because it resembles it; a circle represents a face because, by convention, it stands for a face. However, depiction is not *mere* convention; some ways of depicting a given subject are better than others. When we perceive a pictorial representation of a given subject, according to Gombrich, we have a visual experience that is similar to our seeing the actual subject; depiction is a kind of illusion.

According to Richard WOLLHEIM, perceiving a pictorial representation is not like perceiving the subject depicted. Depiction rests on our natural human capacity to see one thing *in* another. For example, we can see Perry the Platypus in a cloud or the Virgin Mary in a pizza. Seeing a picture as depicting something is an experience Wollheim calls "seeing-in." What we see *in* a painting is the subject represented. However, we see not only what is depicted; we are simultaneously aware of the painting's surface features (brush strokes, and so on), which would obviously not be a part of our experience of the subject itself. Thus, the experience possesses what Wollheim calls "twofoldness," twofold seeing. Kendall WALTON'S view of artistic representation holds that it is a kind of game of make-believe in which paintings, novels, and films are props that prescribe what we are to imagine. A painting represents a chocolate soufflé, say, if it guides us, prompts us, to imagine that we are seeing a soufflé. (Walton suggests that the prop and imagining aspects of his account explain the "twofoldness" of Wollheim's seeing-in.)

On Nelson GOODMAN'S view, a painting represents a seascape by *standing for* a seascape, by being a symbol for, referring to a seascape. Counter to intuition, Goodman argues that resemblance is neither sufficient nor necessary for pictorial representation; pictorial representation, like linguistic representation, rests on denotation. Going further than Gombrich, Goodman claims that representations are *arbitrary* signs or symbols that denote by convention. Thus, there are no right or wrong ways of representing this or that subject matter. We experience these depictions as resemblances simply because we are familiar with them, we are inculcated into the conventions.

Of course, construing representation as depiction does not yield a definition of art because some art forms (and even some paintings) do not depict anything (depiction is not a necessary condition of art). In addition, many kinds of objects that are not works of art are depictions (depiction is not a sufficient condition of art). Stretching the notion of representation, we might construe representation as "aboutness." A work of art represents if it is about something. Arthur DANTO argues that an artifact can possess aboutness not due to perceptual properties but due to a historical and theoretical context, and so on. As a result, two artifacts that look the same can possess a different meaning.

Further Reading

Goldman, A. (2005), "Representation in art," in D. M. Lopes and B. Gaut (eds), *The Routledge Companion to Aesthetics*. London and New York: Routledge Press.

Gombrich, E. H. (1960), *Art and Illusion: A Study in the Psychology of Pictorial Representation* (2nd edn). New York and Princeton, NJ: Princeton University Press.

Lopes, D. (1996), *Understanding Pictures*. Oxford: Oxford University Press.

Walton, K. (1984), "Transparent pictures." *Critical Inquiry*, 11: 246–77.

Sublime

In a handbook on rhetoric entitled *On the Sublime* (written in the first century CE, attributed to Longinus), the author maintains that great works of literature are *hūpsous*; the Greek term means "elevated" or "sublime." A sublime literary work is uplifting and transporting. Some important constituents of the sublime include extraordinary subject matter, writing in a grand, elevated style, and the use of figurative language. Prefiguring later discussions of the sublime, Longinus also refers to astonishing phenomena in nature as sublime, such as a mighty river.

The sublime came to be a kind of sister concept to BEAUTY in the eighteenth century; beauty has to do with more ordered and tame aspects of art and nature, whereas the sublime has to do with more awe-inspiring or terrifying aspects. Drawing upon Joseph Addison's view, Edmund Burke (1729–97), in his *A Philosophical Enquiry into the Origin of Our Ideas of the Sublime and Beautiful* (1757), offers a contrast between beauty and sublimity in empirical terms. According to Burke, objects that are familiar and easily comprehended by us are a source of pleasure, and are considered beautiful. These are objects that, so to speak, submit to us. The contrast is with objects that are surprising, potentially dangerous, painful, terrible, and which are in some sense obscure, presenting a challenge to our perceptual faculties. As long as we are not in actual danger, undergoing pain, we admire such objects, submit to them, and they produce in us a kind of awed delight; such objects are sublime. A work of art may contain beautiful or sublime elements; in some cases, complex works may possess both.

By far, the most influential account of the sublime is Immanuel KANT'S. According to Kant, sublimnity is not a quality of objects but of our responses to certain awesome, natural objects, such as a hurricane or the "starry heavens." A famous passage from Kant's works speaks to this awe or reverence; "Two things fill the mind with ever new and increasing admiration and reverence, the more often and more steadily one reflects on them: *the starry heavens above me and the moral law within me*" (Kant 1997, p. 133). (This statement eventually made it to Kant's tombstone.)

Kant distinguishes between the mathematically sublime, which has to do with vastness, and the dynamically sublime, which has to do with power. Regarding the mathematically sublime, it can be overwhelming to be struck by the fact that we cannot grasp, in one perception, the magnitude of the starry heavens or of a great desert; this can be frustrating and a source of displeasure. This displeasure becomes a pleasurable experience of the sublime in the realization that we are, indeed, able to grasp such magnitudes through reason, through the idea of infinity. In this experience, we are reminded of the power of our faculty of reason (a supersensible faculty at the core of Kant's moral theory). Similarly, in the face of the destructive power of a hurricane or volcano, a case of the dynamically sublime, we experience fear. But if we are in a position of safety, our faculty of reason enables us to detach ourselves from this fear. In such cases, we experience pleasure in the realization that we have the ability, via reason, to set ourselves apart from the powers of nature and our initial fears.

Both judgments of the sublime and judgments of beauty are AESTHETIC JUDGMENTS; both kinds of judgments rest on a pleasurable experience, both are DISINTERESTED, and in both cases, we expect others will agree (both demand universal assent). But there are differences; for example, beauty involves an object's form; sublimnity involves an object's formlessness; in addition, beauty involves the understanding; sublimnity involves reason. See KANT, *CRITIQUE OF JUDGMENT*.

Further Reading

Burke, E. (1958 [1757, 1759]), *A Philosophical Enquiry into the Origin of Our Ideas of the Sublime and the Beautiful*, J. T. Boulton (ed.). London: Routledge and Kegan Paul.
Kant, I. (1987 [1790]), *Critique of Judgment*, W. Pluhar (trans.). Indianapolis: Hackett.
—(1997 [1788]), *Critique of Practical Reason*, M. Gregor (ed. and trans.). Cambridge: Cambridge University Press.
Longinus (1899), *Longinus on the Sublime: The Greek Text Edited after the Paris Manuscript*, W. Rhys Roberts (ed. and trans.). Cambridge: Cambridge University Press.

Taste, see Aesthetic Judgment

Value of Art

We wonder about what art *is* (in the sense of DEFINING ART and in the ONTOLOGICAL sense). We argue about which INTERPRETATION of a novel or film is better, which work of art clarifies a particular EMOTION more thoroughly; and so on. What underlies these endeavors is that art is important to us—why? In what way is art valuable? Perhaps what distinguishes a philosophical theory of art from a mere definition is that while a definition need not weigh-in on art's value, a theory should. When a philosopher claims that the value of art, in general, lies in *x*—whether this is the experience of a certain sort of pleasure, the expression of emotions, or whatever—that account should provide a foundation for evaluating individual works. Secondary considerations may emerge, but one would expect the *x* to provide an anchor for individual evaluations. We would not expect Clive Bell, for instance, to transition from maintaining that artistic value rests wholly on art's form to evaluating individual paintings in terms of their moral messages, nor even their originality. (See BELL, *ART*; FORMALISM; AESTHETIC JUDGMENT).

The oldest and most basic view of art's value is that perceiving art is pleasurable. PLATO believes that we derive pleasure from BEAUTY and artistic imitations (see REPRESENTATION) but he famously worries about the potential negative effects. ARISTOTLE agrees that artistic imitation is pleasurable but he also stresses two additional values of art. First, in his writing on Greek tragedy, he claims that viewing it is CATHARTIC; potentially disruptive emotions, such as fear and pity, are aroused but also purged in the viewing experience. Thus, art can contribute to our psychological well-being (for another interpretation of catharsis, see ARISTOTLE, *POETICS*). Second, Aristotle highlights a cognitive value in tragedy; through its representations of specific characters and their actions, tragedy can convey general truths about human affairs. Both of these points can be extended to other art forms. At the unification of the arts in the eighteenth century, imitation and beauty are central, and pleasure remains connected to both (see the introduction).

In David HUME's influential account of aesthetic judgment, at the core is an agreeable, subjective reaction (pleasure) to a perceptual experience of a work of art. Immanuel KANT also reveals one aspect of what he takes to be art's value (a kind of pleasure) through his account of aesthetic judgment. Notice that if one aims to locate the value of art in the pleasurable experiences it affords, then it is important to distinguish the pleasure associated with works of art from other pleasures, such as the sensuous, bodily pleasures. Kant explores this issue in relation to the notion of the AESTHETIC. One influential idea he develops is that aesthetic pleasure, pleasure in the beautiful, is not the pleasure of gratifying our senses (with, for example, a sweet-tasting food); aesthetic pleasure is DISINTERESTED. In aesthetic experiences, we are occupied with a beautiful object in a contemplative manner *for its own sake*. (See Pierre BOURDIEU for a criticism of disinterest.)

There is another well-known consideration of these issues in moral philosophy, in the writing on utilitarianism by Jeremy Bentham (1748–1832) and John Stuart Mill (1806–73). Utilitarianism, a theory about what makes an action moral, is ultimately grounded on happiness, which is identified with pleasure. Jeremy Bentham argues that there are no qualitative distinctions between different pleasures; pleasure is pleasure. If this is right, if pleasurable experiences can be valued only in terms of the *quantity* of pleasure, then the arts are no more valuable than anything else that can generate an equal quantity of pleasure (games, drugs, sex, food, and so on); art is replaceable. To avoid the criticism that utilitarianism turns on nothing but sensuous pleasure, and is therefore "a doctrine worthy of swine," Mill develops the idea that there is a "lower" kind of pleasure and a "higher" kind of pleasure. Lower pleasures are the sensuous pleasures; higher pleasures are intellectual pleasures. Higher pleasure is intrinsically more valuable than lower pleasure. According to Mill, the pleasure associated with poetry is an example of a higher pleasure. On such a view, certain arts are valuable insofar as they afford the opportunity to experience a higher kind of intellectual pleasure. However, if this intellectual pleasure is interchangeable with other intellectual pleasures, we still have a problem regarding the replaceability of works of art. Below, we will return to the cognitive value of art, and to the question as to whether art's value is instrumental.

According to G. W. F. HEGEL, art's core value lies not at the level of individual perceivers but at the cultural level. Art is valuable in that the best art can convey a culture's worldview, an epoch's ethos. Worldviews change from epoch to epoch, and different art forms are better at expressing different worldviews. Thus, art cannot be evaluated in a vacuum; historical context is crucial in understanding art's value, the value of the art forms, and individual works. Consider the familiar but much more modest claim that works of art give us useful information in ways that a book or newspaper cannot, or lead us to understand a phenomenon in a new way. For example, a rap song may be valued for informing a wide audience, in an engaging and emotionally effective manner, about what it is like to live in a very violent neighborhood, where the inhabitants are without hope; consider Public Enemy's "911 Is a Joke" (*Fear of a Black Planet*, Def Jam, 1990).

MARXISTS maintain that art (and other components of a cultural superstructure, such as philosophy and religion) is shaped, to one degree or another, by the economic conditions of a society, the substructure. Marxists emphasize art's sociopolitical value. If a work of art is merely pleasing, merely entertaining, it will not aid a spectator in becoming aware of, or doing anything about, the injustices she faces under capitalism. On the contrary, the work will function as a palliative, which ultimately reinforces the status quo. Such works of art are not valuable. This line of thought typically leads Marxists to be critical of POPULAR ART (but see Walter BENJAMIN for a contrasting view). Some works of art, however, may be considered valuable even though they merely reflect the economic conditions, if they highlight the substructure in a way that may lead a spectator toward critically examining her situation. Theodor W. ADORNO values art that challenges a listener—art that requires thoughtful engagement. Such art cultivates a critical habit of mind, which predisposes a person also to be critical of her sociopolitical circumstances.

Immanuel Kant, in articulating a disinterested pleasure that grounds aesthetic judgment, is describing something like an AESTHETIC EXPERIENCE. A number of subsequent philosophers have argued that art is valuable due to the experiences it affords, while resisting the notion that these experiences can be described in terms of pleasure. For example, among other dimensions, John DEWEY contends that aesthetic experiences have a pervasive quality, and end in a consummation (see BEARDSLEY).

FORMALISTS, such as Clive BELL and Eduard Hanslick, believe that the essence of visual art and music (respectively) is "significant form" or "beautiful form." The value of works of art lies in their form. But subsequent philosophers have shown that it is difficult to isolate form from content in this way, and it is particularly difficult to specify what makes particular cases of form special. Bell attempts this by maintaining that we know a form to be significant when it arouses the "aesthetic emotion," but this seems to bring us back to a special kind of pleasure or aesthetic experience. Bell defines neither significant form nor the aesthetic emotion independently.

SCHOPENHAUER views human life as essentially one of suffering; one reason art is valuable is that it can provide temporary respite. More importantly, art has cognitive value; we can attain knowledge of Plato's forms ("Ideas") through art. Music is special for Schopenhauer; through music, we can come to know ultimate reality itself, that is, what he refers to as the Will. In his early work, Friedrich NIETZSCHE'S worldview is similar to Schopenhauer's, but Nietzsche describes art and the aesthetic in even more positive terms, as life-affirming; as he famously states in *The Birth of Tragedy*, "Only as an *aesthetic phenomenon* is existence and the world eternally *justified*" (1999, p. 33). One noteworthy suggestion of the later Nietzsche, regarding art's value, is that we can model fine-tuning our own character upon art; we can give ourselves a style.

In addition to the emotion-related value mentioned above in relation to Aristotle, many philosophers have claimed that art is valuable insofar as it has the capacity to EXPRESS emotions. The novelist Leo Tolstoy held that just as speech communicates ideas, art communicates EMOTIONS. An artist, while experiencing an emotion, embodies this emotion in her work. In successful cases, a spectator is "infected" by the emotion. Art is valuable due to this expressive capacity and its ability to unify people by means of such works. R. G. COLLINGWOOD'S expression theory de-emphasizes the spectator and emphasizes the way in which an artist can clarify her emotions in a work of art. An artist begins to work with a vaguely understood emotion, and through the work, she clarifies for herself what she is feeling. Thus, for Collingwood, one value of art is that it can help an artist to better understand herself. Art can also aid in a spectator's self-understanding; a spectator may not understand clearly what he is feeling, or has felt, until he finds it articulated in a work of art. Moreover, art can expand our emotional repertoire.

Martin Heidegger holds that the best works of art can create new cultural paradigms; they can open up a "world" that grounds new ways of understanding things, events, actions, and so on. For example, he claims that a Greek temple *gathers* the world of Greek culture and religion; it *unifies* what nearly everything means for that culture. This value of art has to do with art's capacity to render things intelligible, to bestow meaning, to create new possibilities of meaning. See HEIDEGGER, "THE ORIGIN OF THE WORK OF ART."

Note that some accounts of art's value above seem to construe works of art as *instrumentally* valuable; others seem to take works of art to be valuable *intrinsically*, as ends in themselves. Formalism seems to be in the latter group (but philosophers have even questioned whether formalism can claim that art has strictly intrinsic value).

We should be worried about an instrumental account of art's value because, in such a case, works of art will be replaceable by other items; for example, if art is valuable because works of art give us sensuous pleasure, then a given work of art is replaceable by anything else (a drug, say) which gives us the same quantity of pleasure. Here is one way out of this troubling situation. Consider accounts in which works of art seem to be valued instrumentally (e.g., take theories that base art's value on aesthetic experience); it may be the case that each work of art affords a *unique* experience that no other object or work of art can provide. If this is right, then perhaps each work of art is unique and irreplaceable. Can we make the same maneuver regarding theories such as Hegel's or Adorno's?

When philosophers ask about art's value, notice the kinds of answers that we are *not* looking for, and notice that the following answers make art's value merely instrumental. Paintings by Van Gogh, Cezanne, and so on, are valuable as financial investments. Some works of art are religiously valuable in that they perform the function of introducing spectators to religious stories and themes. Some psychologists draw upon the therapeutic value of art. A song adopted as a theme song for a political campaign can be politically valuable (contrast this latter kind of value with Adorno's view).

Further Reading

Budd, M. (1995), *Values of Art: Painting, Poetry, and Music*. London: Penguin.

Goldman, A. (1995), *Aesthetic Value*. Boulder: Westview Press.

Nietzsche, F. (1999 [1872]), *The Birth of Tragedy*, R. Guess and R. Speirs (eds), R. Speirs (trans.). Cambridge: Cambridge University Press.

Smith, B. H. (1988), *Contingencies of Value: Alternative Perspectives for Critical Theory*. Cambridge, MA: Harvard University Press.

Key Thinkers

Adorno, Theodor W. (1903–69)

Adorno was a German philosopher and leading member of the Frankfurt School of Critical Theory. He studied and taught at Frankfurt University until the rise of the Nazi party; he subsequently lived in exile in England, and then in the United States, returning to Frankfurt in 1949. To obtain an initial orientation to his work, note that Adorno was heavily influenced by G. W. F. HEGEL and MARXISM, and was critical of Immanuel KANT.

A rigid strain of Marxism conceives of ideology (a society's superstructure, which includes philosophy and the arts) as *determined* by the substructure (the economic base of a society). On such a view, the superstructure *reflects* the substructure and does not influence it. Adorno embraces a strain of Marxism, according to which the superstructure can, indeed, influence the substructure. According to Adorno, art's value lies not in its BEAUTY, its expressive potential, nor in its capacity to afford AESTHETIC EXPERIENCES; rather, art's value lies in its ability to function as a vehicle for readers, listeners, and so on, to become aware of, and to critically examine their existing sociopolitical circumstances.

In order to acquire such critical leverage, art must first attain distance from the practical realm. Counter to ordinary intuitions, truly political art cannot serve an explicit political or social function (at a state event or a protest gathering, for instance); that is, art must be autonomous. Art that wears its social message on its sleeve, so to speak, is too involved with the current milieu; this is the orientation of mere propaganda. By attaining this distance, this autonomy, art exemplifies a refusal to serve a social function.

Adorno not only eschews the beautiful and the aesthetically pleasing, he holds that truly political, progressive art is dissonant, disturbing, and demands thoughtful engagement. He praises the avant-garde (atonal music over tonal classical music, for example), and in general, he is critical of the POPULAR ARTS such as jazz and Hollywood films (see BENJAMIN for a contrasting view). According to Adorno, popular works of art are not politically neutral; they are ideological; they are commodities that dull our critical inclinations and foster both artistic and sociopolitical conformism. Contrariwise, avant-garde art refuses to be defined or valued in terms of exchange value; by being experientially difficult, it resists commodification. Avant-garde art's intellectually challenging nature fosters in audiences independent thinking and a critical disposition, which predisposes them to be socially and politically critical.

Adorno favored instrumental music and abstract art generally, prioritizing form over content (see FORMALISM). Such art must be attended to *for itself*; in this way, its mere existence models freedom. Art achieves this freedom in virtue of what Adorno calls its truth-content. This notion of truth is obviously not the traditional notion of a representation that tracks reality (on Adorno's view, accurately representing reality would be to represent the oppressive state of affairs obtaining in society); rather, art that satisfies Adorno's notion of truth attains sufficient distance from social reality (it resists inauthenticity, resists becoming commodified) and serves as a vehicle for critiquing society.

Some artists make creative decisions dictated only by the demands of the art's medium, and according to the demands of the particular work of art, but even such art is not autonomous in the sense of being interpretable and evaluatable from an ahistorical perspective. Art's nature and value is historically and socially situated. For example, the atonal music Adorno favored was not better than tonal music as such but only within the historical context resulting from, as Adorno sees it, the failures of composers in the tonal tradition.

Further Reading

Adorno, T. W. (1967), "On the fetish-character in music and the regression of listening," in *The Essential Frankfurt School Reader*, A. Arato and E. Gebhart (eds). New York: Urizen Books.

Adorno, T. W. (1976), *Introduction to the Sociology of Music*. E. B. Ashton (trans), Continuum.

—(1997), *Aesthetic Theory*, G. Adorno and R. Tiedemann (eds), Minneapolis: University Of Minnesota Press.

Goehr, L. (1994), "Political Music and the Politics of Music," in P. Alperson (ed.), *The Philosophy of Music*, Special Issue of *Journal of Aesthetics and Art Criticism*, 52(1): 99–112.

Aristotle

Aristotle (384–322 B.C.E.), along with his teacher PLATO, is one of most influential philosophers in the Western tradition. Aristotle entered Plato's Academy in his late teens, remaining there for 20 years, leaving only after Plato's death. He later established his own school in Athens, The Lyceum. Aristotle produced seminal texts on an extremely wide range of topics: metaphysics, ethics, politics, biology, logic, meteorology, psychology, and the philosophy of art, to name only a few. Aristotle is also known for being a tutor of the young Alexander the Great.

Aristotle's approach was generally empirical, especially as contrasted with Plato's rationalism. His principal work in philosophy of art is his *Poetics*, which focuses on tragedy. In this small book, Aristotle offers an account of what tragedy is, explaining how it differs from other arts. In addition, although he does not mention Plato in the *Poetics*, Aristotle outlines what are often taken to be responses to Plato's criticisms of tragedy (see *Plato, REPUBLIC*). Plato was famously worried that the arts stir the emotions in spectators, empowering spectators' emotions at the expense of their reason. Aristotle maintains that tragedy has a therapeutic effect on spectators; the spectators undergo a catharsis, which, according to the traditional interpretation, is a kind of purging. This is a venting of emotions, such as fear and pity, which otherwise may be disruptive. Plato also criticized the arts for not conveying knowledge. Aristotle claims that tragedy does, indeed, possess cognitive value; we can learn from poetry; through its depiction of specific characters and their actions, poetry can convey general truths about human affairs. For a more detailed discussion, see ARISTOTLE, POETICS. The curious reader may also want to look at Aristotle's *Politics*, book VIII, where he discusses catharsis and other relevant issues, as well as his *Nicomachean Ethics*, book IV.

Further Reading

Barnes, J. (ed.) (1984), *The Complete Works of Aristotle*, Volumes I and II. Princeton, NJ: Princeton University Press.
Ross, W. D. (1923), *Aristotle*. London: Methuen and Co.

Barthes, Roland (1915–80)

Barthes was a French theorist and critic who wrote on literature, culture, photography, and so on; his work was multidimensional and evolving. The core of his poststructuralist position on literature is as follows. Traditionally, the author is seen as the origin and anchor of a work's meaning. The author fixes the meaning of the work (on this view, we have what Barthes calls a "work"). The structuralist view dispenses with the author but maintains that the meaning of the text is fixed, due to its structure. A structuralist can proclaim the "death of the author," but a text still has a determinate meaning that is presented as the goal of INTERPRETATION. The poststructuralist maneuver comes in the claim that once we discard the author as a fixer of the work's meaning, then there is no sense in supposing that there is only one meaning. In contrast to a "work," the meaning of what Barthes calls a "text" is open. A text is produced by the activity of a *reader*. The reader, like an author, creates meaning. Barthes distinguishes between "readerly," interpretations of a text (the reader is passive), and "writerly" interpretations (the reader is active, creative). Authors of writerly texts look upon the reader's interpretation as a part of the work.

In his *Camera Lucida* (1980), Barthes sets out an influential manner of conceiving of the content of photographs, drawing a distinction between two themes or aspects of photographs: the *studium* and the *punctum*. The studium consists of a photograph's culturally coded, symbolic meanings, which are available to an average viewer; this is its manifest, obvious meaning. The punctum consists of a feature (or features) of a photograph that punctuate the studium, a detail in the photograph that disrupts the obvious meaning of a photograph, and which has a decisive effect upon the viewer. Regarding the punctum, Barthes writes, "It is this element which rises from the scene, shoots out of it like an arrow, and pierces me" (26). A part of what makes the punctum so effective is that it is an element of a photograph that does not fit; it is not intelligible from within the standard symbolism, and in some sense, it eludes understanding. Later in *Camera Lucida*, Barthes articulates another punctum; it is not a mere detail in a photograph but concerns the way in which photographs present objects to us both as present, and at the same time, as being in the past ("that-has-been").

Further Reading

Barthes, R. (1975 [1970]), *S/Z*, R. Miller (trans.). London: Cape.
—(1978), *Image-Music-Text*, S. Heath (trans.). New York: Hill and Wang.
—(1980), *Camera Lucida*, R. Howard (trans.). New York: Hill and Wang.

Beardsley, Monroe (1915–85)

Beardsley, an American philosopher, was easily one of the most important figures in twentieth-century analytic philosophy of art. He taught at Swarthmore College, Temple University, and elsewhere. Early in his career, he co-authored, with W. K. Wimsatt, two influential essays on literature, which were aligned with New Criticism: "The Intentional Fallacy" (1946) and "The Affective Fallacy" (1949). Beardsley and his co-author argue that neither a writer's intentions nor a reader's affective responses are relevant to the INTERPRETATION and evaluation of a literary work. Beardsley later extended these claims beyond the one art form. Consider this reasoning regarding the intentionally fallacy—if an artist's intended meaning is *not* successfully realized in a work of art, then her intentions are not instructive in uncovering the meaning or evaluating the work; if her intended meaning *is* realized in the work, then we can disregard those intentions and simply focus on the work. An important consideration for Beardsley is that the work is public and available for examination, whereas an artist's intentions are private. It is instructive to note the common ground between Beardsley and the poststructuralists, Roland BARTHES and Jacques Derrida (1930–2004): all agree that the meaning of a literary text is not fixed by its author. However, Barthes and Derrida deny that a text possesses any fixed meaning at all; Beardsley holds that it does.

In his 1958 book, *Aesthetics: Problems in the Philosophy of Criticism*, Beardsley approaches the philosophy of art as meta-criticism, an examination of the concepts and argumentative methods of art critics. Beardsley is often singled out for his views on AESTHETIC EXPERIENCE. In this early work, his account of aesthetic experience is similar to John DEWEY's: aesthetic experience is complex, intense and unified. Later, in *The Aesthetic Point of View* (1982), he acknowledges that many experiences have an aesthetic character but lack the unity required to classify them as aesthetic experiences. His account of the broader notion of *the aesthetic in experience* (i.e., experience with aesthetic character) is set out in terms of five criteria. He takes the first criterion, object directedness, to be necessary. Any three of the final four criteria are necessary—felt freedom, detached affect, active discovery, and wholeness.

Beardsley's often-discussed definition of art is functional, and offered in terms of his later view of the aesthetic in experience: a work of art is an artifact ("an arrangement of conditions") intended to afford "an experience with marked aesthetic character" (see his 1982). Works of art are valuable insofar as they afford "aesthetic gratification." Which kind of gratification is aesthetic is determined by the properties of the *object* of experience rather than the properties of the experience itself; Beardsley's earlier view focused on properties of the experience itself. The properties of the object Beardsley is referring to are formal properties and what he calls "regional qualities." See AESTHETIC PROPERTIES, CREATIVITY, INTERPRETATION, and LITERATURE.

Further Reading

Beardsley, M. C. (1981), *Aesthetics: Problems in the Philosophy of Criticism*. Indianapolis: Hackett.
—(1982), *The Aesthetic Point of View*, M. Wreen and D. Callen (eds). Ithaca, NY: Cornell University Press.
Iseminger, G. (2005), "Aesthetic experience," in J. Levinson (ed.), *The Oxford Handbook of Aesthetics*. Oxford and New York: Oxford University Press.
Wimsatt, W. K. and Beardsley, M. C. (1946), "The intentional fallacy," *Sewanee Review*, 54: 468–88.

Bell, Clive (1881–1964)

A British art critic and member of the Bloomsbury Group, Bell's book, *Art*, sets out a FORMALIST theory of visual art. He offers an essential definition of visual art in terms of what he calls "significant form" (see DEFINING ART). We know when we are perceiving a work of art with significant form, according to Bell, because it arouses the "aesthetic emotion." See BELL, *ART*; AESTHETIC EXPERIENCE; EMOTION. For further reading, see the entry on Bell's *Art*.

Benjamin, Walter (1892–1940)

A German MARXIST philosopher and critical theorist, Benjamin wrote extensively on literature, but his most influential essay in the philosophy of art, by far, is "The Work of Art in the Age of Its Technical Reproducibility" (1936; reprinted in *Illuminations*). Although the reproduction of works of art is not new (consider apprentices learning by copying, consider woodcuts, and so on), as a result of the modern technical reproducibility of photography, recorded music, and film, these arts do not have the "aura" of traditional arts such as painting and sculpture. This aura is a quality of our experience of these traditional objects; we experience these objects as possessing a reverential, mysterious dimension; they are distant and unapproachable; this is due to their singularity, uniqueness, and authenticity.

Benjamin emphasizes the positive ramifications of the evaporation of aura. Technological reproduction enables works of art to engage viewers within their own environments, no longer in museums and concert halls alone. This is an emancipation for art and spectators; art is freed from tradition and location. This allows for new ways of experiencing works of art, and new political forms of art. Traditional ways of engaging with art emphasize ideas such as eternal value, mystery, genius, and ritual; Benjamin, a Marxist, sees this tradition as associated with capitalism, and as paving the way for fascism. Mass art, in contrast, possesses a liberating, politically critical, and progressive potential. As art moves away from the ritualistic model, spectators are released from their reverential engagement; they are permitted a critical distance. Furthermore, popular art opens us up to engaging communally; seeing a film at a movie theater, for example, is a communal experience. Contrast Benjamin's view of the political benefit of popular art with Theodor W. ADORNO's negative view of popular art. Adorno maintains that popular art, being mere entertainment, discourages critical thought, political engagement, and it breeds conformism. See POPULAR ART, FILM, and PHOTOGRAPHY.

Further Reading

Benjamin, W. (1968), *Illuminations: Essays and Reflections*, H. Arendt (ed.). New York: Harcourt, Brace & World.

—(1999), *The Arcades Project*, H. Eiland and K. McLaughlin (trans.). Cambridge, MA: Harvard University Press.

Friedlander, E. (2012), *Walter Benjamin: A Philosophical Portrait*. Cambridge and London: Harvard University Press.

Bourdieu, Pierre (1930–2002)

Bourdieu was a French sociologist who was influenced by MARXISM, existentialism, and structuralism, and whose work has had a steadily increasing influence on the philosophy of art. In explaining social phenomena, he seeks a middle path between the subjectivism of existentialism and the objectivism of certain strains of Marxism and structuralism. Bourdieu takes the predominant view of art to be that works of art are autonomous objects that can only be recognized as such through DISINTERESTED perception, emphasizing FORM over content (this is Bourdieu's interpretation of Immanuel KANT). Far from how Kant saw his own analysis, Bourdieu sees it as a mere description of how those in Kant's elite social class approached and understood art, which Kant then presented as a universal, objective philosophy of art and AESTHETIC JUDGMENT.

Bourdieu calls the aptitude for understanding and perceiving art in these Kantian terms "the aesthetic disposition"; a person who possesses this competency has "taste." This view of taste has deep sociopolitical implications. Based in part on surveys conducted in France in the 1960s and the 1970s, Bourdieu concluded that taste is much more prevalent in individuals with bourgeois origins, and much less prevalent in working-class individuals. Taste is cultivated through an elite education and a bourgeois home life, but the bourgeoisie treat taste as if it were a natural gift.

Bourdieu also notices a related difference between the kind of art preferred by the working-class and the art preferred by the bourgeoisie. Working-class art emphasizes content (consider American examples such as the importance of plot in Hollywood movies, and the importance of stories in classic rock songs, for instance, those of Bob Seger and Bruce Springsteen). Bourgeois art emphasizes form (consider abstract art and instrumental classical music). Given these differences, taste serves as a *mark of distinction*. It is possible to determine which class a person belongs to by determining which kinds of art she prefers. Moreover, preferences in art *justify* one's class status, because taste is required to appreciate the finer things in life (fine furniture, fine food, haute couture, and so on). If a person does not have taste, then there is justification for her not having *access* to the finer things. It is in this sense that taste can function as a tool of domination.

According to Bourdieu, the working-class preferences for certain music, films, novels, and so on—the working-class "aesthetic"— is not a true aesthetic; it is defined negatively in contrast to the bourgeois aesthetic. The problem rests on the emphasis in POPULAR ART on content at the expense of form. Bourdieu has been criticized both for misunderstanding popular art and for misunderstanding Kant; see, for example, Richard Shusterman (1992) and Theodore Gracyk (2007).

Further Reading

Bourdieu, P. (1987), "The historical genesis of a pure aesthetic." *Journal of Aesthetics and Art Criticism*, vol. 46, *Analytic Aesthetics*, 201–10.
—(1989 [1979]), *Distinction: A Social Critique of the Judgment of Taste*, R. Nice (trans.). Cambridge, MA: Harvard University Press.
—(1993), *The Field of Cultural Production: Essays on Art and Literature*, R. Johnson (ed.). New York: Columbia University Press.
Gracyk, T. (2007), *Listening to Popular Music: Or, How I Learned to Stop Worrying and Love Led Zeppelin*. Ann Arbor: University of Michigan Press.
Grenfell, M. (2008), *Pierre Bourdieu Key Concepts*. Durham: Acumen Publishing.
Shusterman, R. (2000), *Pragmatist Aesthetics: Living Beauty, Rethinking Art* (2nd edn). Lanham: Rowman & Littlefield.

Collingwood, Robin George (1889–1943)

A British philosopher, Collingwood wrote in a number of areas of philosophy, often pursuing different philosophical intuitions from his British contemporaries. He wrote on the philosophy of history, metaphysics, philosophy of art, and so on. In his THE PRINCIPLES OF ART, Collingwood draws an influential distinction between art and craft, puts forward an idealist ONTOLOGY, and most importantly, lays out his expression theory of art, which is heavily influenced by the Italian philosopher Bendetto Croce (1866–1952). See DEFINING ART, EMOTION, CREATIVITY, INTERPRETATION, ONTOLOGY, VALUE OF ART, and DEWEY, *ART AS EXPERIENCE*.

Further Reading

Collingwood, R. G. (1994), *The Idea of History*. Oxford University Press.
Krausz, M. (1972), *Critical Essays on the Philosophy of R. G. Collingwood*. Oxford: Clarendon, pp. 42–65.
Ridley, Aaron (1997), "Not Ideal: Collingwood's Expression Theory," *Journal of Aesthetics and Art Criticism*, 55: 263–72.

Danto, Arthur Coleman (b. 1924)

Danto is an American philosopher whose work has surely been shaped by living in New York City. In 1964, he was struck by Andy Warhol's *Brillo Box*, struck by the fact that the boxes were perceptually indistinguishable from their supermarket soap pad counterparts. More importantly, he developed this observation into a theory of art (see DEFINING ART). Danto reasons that whichever property or properties distinguish the work of art, *Brillo Box*, from the nonartwork Brillo boxes must be imperceptible, nonexhibited. Danto's definition of art turns on nonexhibited properties.

According to Danto, works of art are artifacts that are *about* something; that is, works of art embody a meaning (*Brillo Box*, for instance, is about the nature of art). Further, works of art express a point of view about their meaning, and they present this point of view elliptically (METAPHORICALLY); the point of view must be deciphered. Thus, determining a work of art's meaning and point of view requires INTERPRETATION. Importantly, an interpretation must be informed by the art theory that is appropriate to the work's location in history. The historical dimension of Danto's theory is central: accurately making sense of a work of art's meaning requires correctly identifying the art-historical context within which it was made. This role of the art-historical context in Danto's definition of art entails that a work of art such as *Brillo Box* could not have been a work of art in a period in which the theories are markedly different, for example, in the nineteenth century. These are the principal components of Danto's theory, which is an essential definition of art, and which is also, as we have seen, historicist. Danto's "end of art" thesis maintains that art history ends with Warhol's *Brillo Boxes;* this wraps up the final period of art. Art history is teleological, directed toward a goal. Each period aims at its own goal and ends when that goal is achieved. See HEGEL, G. W. F, *LECTURES ON FINE ART.* In the Renaissance period, for example, visual artists strove toward increasingly accurate representations. The goal of the final, modernist period of art is self-definition (seeking after the nature of art). Warhol's *Brillo Box* takes this endeavor as far as art can, by formulating the question about the nature of art in terms of indiscernible counterparts. Subsequently, it is up to philosophers (Danto, in fact) to finish the definitional project. The point is not that there can be no art after Warhol but that there is no longer a teleological, art-historical narrative; in this posthistorical, pluralist environment, anything goes. The essay in which Danto first grapples with Warhol is "The Artworld" (1964). His magnum opus is *The Transfiguration of the Commonplace* (1981). See DEFINING ART, CONCEPTUAL ART, and DANCE.

Further Reading

Carroll, N. (1993). "Essence, expression, and history: Arthur Danto's philosophy of art," in M. Rollins (ed.), *Danto and his Critics.* Oxford: Basil Blackwell.
Danto, A. C. (1964), "The artworld," *Journal of Philosophy*, 61: 571–84.
—(1984), "The End of Art," in B. Lang (ed.), *The Death of Art.* New York: Haven, pp. 5–35.
—(1986), *The Transfiguration of the Commonplace.* Cambridge, MA: Harvard University Press, 1981.

Dewey, John (1859–1952)

Along with Charles S. Peirce and William James, Dewey was one of the principal American pragmatists. Although he wrote his dissertation on Kant, Hegel was an early influence. Dewey wrote widely in a number of areas of philosophy, such as logic, the philosophy of education, and political philosophy. Although Dewey discusses art briefly in his *Experience and Nature* (1925), his principal work in the philosophy of art is *Art as Experience* (1934). Dewey's theory, as the title suggests, places AESTHETIC EXPERIENCE at the center of the phenomenon of art. Although the book was not embraced by the profession during the middle of the twentieth century (due to the dominance of analytic philosophy), in the past couple of decades, it has become increasingly influential. See DEWEY, ART AS EXPERIENCE.

Further Reading

Alexander, T. (1987), *John Dewey's Theory of Art, Experience, and Nature: The Horizons of Feeling*. Albany, NY: State University of New York Press.
Campbell, J. (1995), *Understanding John Dewey*. Chicago, IL: Open Court.
Dewey, J. (1929), *Experience and Nature*. Chicago: Open Court.

Dickie, George (b. 1926)

George Dickie is an American philosopher who articulated fruitful criticisms of the notion of AESTHETIC EXPERIENCE (including criticisms of the aesthetic attitude, see DISINTEREST) in an on-going debate between he and Monroe BEARDSLEY. But Dickie will be remembered primarily for his institutional theory of art. He proposed his institutional theory in the late 1960s, a period during which it became increasingly clear that traditional definitions of art did not accommodate the art of the time. Dickie's is an essential definition of art, consisting of necessary and sufficient conditions for attaining art-status (see DEFINING ART). His theory does not rest on perceivable features or functions of works of art, such as Clive BELL's "significant form" or Beardsley's affordance of aesthetic experience; rather, Dickie's theory rests on the relations between artifacts and the activities of individuals in an *artworld* (drawing upon Arthur

DANTO'S concept). Dickie's theory is classificatory only; it does not address the VALUE OF ART. The aim is only to determine which things are art and which are not.

The institutional theory of art offers a *procedural* definition of art: art status is conferred upon an artifact by a certain procedure, which is grounded in the social practices of an artworld. An artworld is a human institution consisting of artists, an art-going public, art schools, curators, critics, and so on. Uncontroversially, first, works of art are necessarily artifacts. A work of art is an artifact that has the status of "candidate for appreciation" conferred upon (certain aspects of) it by someone acting on behalf of the artworld (usually, the artist). This is analogous to a member of the legal system (a judge, say) conferring marriage-status upon a man and a woman, two women, or two men. Traditional kinds of works of art are artifacts in the normal sense: these are person-made objects. But Dickie also claims that ready-mades and found art are artifacts; artifactuality is conferred by a member of the artworld.

Dickie offers a second version of his theory in his 1984 book, *The Art Circle*. Two important differences are, first, that found art and ready-mades are artifacts in the sense that artists use such objects as artistic media. Second, artwork status is not conferred; it is *achieved* by an artifact's being situated within the artworld: a work of art is "an artifact of a kind created to be presented to an artworld public." One criticism of Dickie's institutional theory of art is that if an artifact is put forward as a candidate for appreciation, it is put forward for a reason; *that reason* is the important factor in determining its art-status, not the social function performed by the artworld member. See CONCEPTUAL ART.

Further Reading

Dickie, G. (1964), "The Myth of the Aesthetic Attitude." *American Philosophical Quarterly*, 1: 55–65.
—(1965), "Beardsley's Phantom Aesthetic Experience." *Journal of Philosophy*, 62: 129–36.
—(1974), *Art and the Aesthetic: An Institutional Analysis*. Ithaca, NY: Cornell University Press.
—(1984), *The Art Circle*. New York: Havens.

Goodman, Nelson (1906–98)

Goodman was an American philosopher who was influential in a number of areas of philosophy in addition to the philosophy of art, for instance, metaphysics and epistemology. In his *Languages of Art* (1968), Goodman offers a theory of works of art as symbols. Painting, music, and the other arts are symbol systems; a symbol system is a collection of symbols governed by syntactic and semantic rules; each system refers to things in its own way; one kind of symbol system is a natural language. Identifying a work of art's symbols, their reference, and so on, is the business of INTERPRETATION. In this entry, we focus on Goodman's influential ideas about pictorial REPRESENTATION, EXPRESSION, an important ONTOLOGICAL distinction, and architecture.

A painting represents a seascape by *standing for* a seascape, by being a symbol for, referring to a seascape. Counter to intuition, Goodman argues that resemblance is neither sufficient nor necessary for pictorial representation; pictorial representation, like linguistic representation, rests on denotation. Representations are arbitrary signs or symbols that denote by convention. Thus, there are no right or wrong ways of representing this or that subject matter. We experience these depictions as resemblances simply because we are familiar with them, we are inculcated into the conventions.

Denotation is one kind of symbolic reference, another is exemplification; a symbol that exemplifies does not refer by denoting but refers to one or more of the properties it possesses (for simplicity's sake, I am ignoring Goodman's nominalism here). Consider a tailor's swatch. While many items of clothing may be made of gabardine, a gabardine swatch is not only made of gabardine (possession), it also refers to gabardine; the swatch is the kind of symbol that exemplifies gabardine. Goodman claims that works of art express emotions and other properties by METAPHORICALLY exemplifying them. Works of art are often said to express emotions and other properties that they do not actually possess; for example, a piece of instrumental music may be said to express longing. Clearly, the piece of music itself is not literally longing for someone, but according to Goodman, the music can possess the property of longing metaphorically.

Regarding ONTOLOGY, Goodman draws an influential distinction between *autographic* and *allographic* art forms. Painting, sculpture, and etchings are examples of autographic art forms; music, literature, theatre, and dance are examples of allographic art forms (architecture is a mixed art form). Notation is at the core of the distinction; autographic art forms do not admit of notation; allographic art forms do. It is instructive to consider forgery. The distinction between an original and a forgery is an important one regarding autographic works, whereas it is not regarding allographic works. As long as my copy of *Moby Dick* contains the same words, and so on, as the original, then it is an instance of *Moby Dick*. As long as a performance of Ravel's *Bolero* complies with the score (with the notation), then it is a performance of that work. (Note, however, that Goodman's claim here is counterintuitive: one small mistake in a performance of *Bolero* means that it fails to be a performance of that work.) Books and performances that do not comply in these ways are not forgeries; they are simply not instances of the given works. The identity of an autographic work depends upon its history of production; a forgery has a different history of production. This distinction is not identical to the distinction between singular and multiple works of art. Singular works and paintings, frescos, noncast sculptures, and so on; multiple works are music, literature, plays, photographs, cast sculptures, and the like. While the Mona Lisa exists only in one place at one time, Beethoven's Fifth Symphony may be performed in multiple locations simultaneously. Although all singular works are autographic, some multiple works are also autographic; etchings and woodcuts, for example, are autographic but multiple. It is important to note the effect of Goodman's nominalism with respect to the ontology of allographic works. A nominalist maintains that abstract objects do not exist; thus, according to Goodman, the musical work (say) is not an abstract structure (and it is also not the score); rather, the musical work is the set of performances that comply with the score.

Architectural works of art are distinguished from mere buildings insofar as they function as symbols. Relatively few architectural works refer by denoting (the Sydney Opera House, for example, denotes sailboats). More commonly, architectural works refer by *exemplifying*. Architectural works may also exemplify METAPHORICALLY, which Goodman calls expression; for example, a building might metaphorically exemplify movement or freedom. INTERPRETING a work of architecture is an attempt to understand its reference. While Goodman denies the importance of the architects' intentions in determining which interpretation is correct, he is not willing to adopt a relativist position—"A Gothic cathedral that soars and sings does not equally droop and grumble." See REPRESENTATION, DANCE.

Further Reading

Elgin, Catherine Z. (ed.) (1997), *Nelson Goodman's Philosophy of Art*. New York: Garland.

Goodman, N. (1976), *Languages of Art*. Indianapolis: Hackett.

—(1978), *Ways of Worldmaking*. Indianapolis: Hackett.

—(1992), "How buildings mean," in P. A. Alperson (ed.), *Philosophy of the Visual Arts*. New York: Oxford University Press, pp. 368–76.

Hegel, Georg Wilhelm Friedrich (1770–1831)

Hegel, a German idealist philosopher, is one of the true seminal figures in philosophy, the root of the continental tradition. A systematic philosopher, Hegel wrote widely on metaphysics, ETHICS, the philosophy of history, and so on. Hegel emphasized that history does not proceed arbitrarily but unfolds rationally, aiming toward the goal of individual human freedom. Hegel claims that the best works of art have the capacity to convey a culture's worldview. His principal work in the philosophy of art consists of lectures that were compiled posthumously: see HEGEL, LECTURES ON FINE ART.

Further Reading

Hegel, G. W. F. (1979), *Phenomenology of Spirit*, A. V. Miller (trans.). Oxford: Oxford University Press.

—(2012), *Introduction to the Philosophy of History*, L. Rauch (trans.). Indianapolis and Cambridge: Hackett.

Taylor, C. (1975), *Hegel*. Cambridge: Cambridge University Press.

Heidegger, Martin (1889–1976)

Heidegger was a student of the founder of PHENOMENOLOGY, Edmund Husserl. Heidegger's most well-known book is *Being and Time* (1927), in which he explores the question of being, through an examination of *dasein* (human being). In his later period, he turns his attention to art in his essay, "The Origin of the Work of Art" (1936). According to Heidegger, works of art have two essential

traits: a work of art sets up a world, and it sets forth the earth. See
HEIDEGGER, "THE ORIGIN OF THE WORK OF ART."

Further Reading

Heidegger, M. (1962 [1927]), *Being and Time*, J. Macquarrie and E.
Robinson (trans.). Oxford: Basil Blackwell.
—(1993), "The question concerning technology," W. Lovitt (trans.) with
revisions by D. F. Krell, in D. F. Krell (ed.), *Martin Heidegger: Basic
Writings* (revised edn). London: Routledge, pp. 311–41.
Dreyfus, H. L. (1990), *Being-in-the-World: A Commentary on Heidegger's
Being and Time, Division I*. Cambridge, MA: MIT Press.

Hume, David (1711–76)

Hume, a Scottish empiricist philosopher, is probably the most
important philosopher to have written in English. Three works
are responsible for this reputation: *A Treatise of Human Nature*
(1739–40), *An Enquiry concerning Human Understanding* (1748),
and *An Enquiry concerning the Principles of Morals* (1751). In
his "On Tragedy" (1757), Hume broaches what is known as "the
paradox of TRAGEDY," which refers to the perplexing fact that we
enjoy experiences of tragic drama even though they center on the
so-called negative EMOTIONS, such as sorrow and anxiety. These
negative emotions, according to Hume, are due to the subject
matter, whereas the pleasure we experience is due to the way in
which the subject matter is REPRESENTED. Thus, the pleasure we
experience is due to the *quality* of a tragedy's construction. When
we experience a tragedy of sufficient quality, the negative emotions
are "converted" into pleasure; the pleasure, in a sense, overpowers
the negative emotions.

Hume's text that is most widely read in philosophy of art
courses is, "Of the Standard of Taste" (1757). In this essay, Hume
tackles the thorny problem of AESTHETIC JUDGMENT. He adopts the
position that beauty is not a property of objects but a matter of
an object's power to produce pleasure in spectators, which means
that aesthetic judgments are based on subjective experiences of
pleasure. Hume's approach to conceiving of aesthetic judgments

as something other than mere personal preferences is to develop the notion of a "true judge." A true judge has certain qualities (considerable experience in comparing works of art, a lack or prejudice, and so on), which make his judgments more decisive than mere opinions. For a more detailed discussion, see HUME, "OF THE STANDARD OF TASTE."

Further Reading

Gracyk, T. (2011), "Hume's aesthetics," in E. N. Zalta (ed.), *The Stanford Encyclopedia of Philosophy*. http://plato.stanford.edu/entries/hume-aesthetics/#HumEssTra/.

Hume, D. (1998), *Enquiry concerning the Principles of Morals*, T. L. Beauchamp (ed.). Oxford and New York: Oxford University Press.

Hume, D. (1999), *An Enquiry Concerning Human Understanding*, T. L. Beauchamp (ed.). Oxford and New York: Oxford University Press.

Stroud, B. (1977), *Hume*. London: Routledge and Kegan Paul.

Kant, Immanuel (1724–1804)

Kant was a German philosopher whose writing on metaphysics, epistemology, moral theory, and politics has made him one of the most important philosophers in the Western tradition. Many students read his *Groundwork of the Metaphysics of Morals* (1785) or venture into his magnum opus, *The Critique of Pure Reason* (1781). Kant's third *Critique*, *The Critique of Judgment* (1790), is considered by many to be the most important text in modern philosophy of art, known for its subtle, multifaceted treatment of AESTHETIC JUDGMENT (a judgment that an object is beautiful). Kant, like David HUME, holds that BEAUTY is not a quality of objects. Kant argues that finding something to be beautiful, asserting an aesthetic judgment, is a matter of subjective experience, but this does not mean that aesthetic judgments are merely subjective preferences. The experience of a specific kind of pleasure grounds aesthetic judgments; this pleasure is due to a harmony of the cognitive powers of the understanding and imagination; this harmony is the result of the perception of certain objects that we call beautiful. These judgments are objective because our cognitive powers are basically the same. For more detail, see KANT, *CRITIQUE*

OF JUDGMENT. Kant also puts forward an influential account of the SUBLIME, distinguishing between the mathematically sublime and the dynamically sublime.

Further Reading

Kant, I. (1998 [1781]), *Critique of Pure Reason*, P. Guyer and A. Wood (eds). Cambridge: Cambridge University Press.
—(1998 [1785]), *Groundwork of the Metaphysics of Morals*, M. Gregor (ed.). New York: Cambridge University Press.
Körner, S. (1955), *Kant*. London: Penguin Books.

Nietzsche, Friedrich (1844–1900)

Nietzsche has been extremely influential within twentieth-century continental philosophy, and his work has been increasingly considered by analytic philosophers. Before encountering Nietzsche, a reader should know that his ideas evolved more than most philosophers; due to these changes, and due to his unorthodox writing style, there seem to be more disagreements among scholars about Nietzsche's claims and arguments than regarding many other philosophers.

In his *The Birth of Tragedy* (1872), Nietzsche proclaims, "Only as an *aesthetic phenomenon* is existence and the world eternally justified." Nietzsche adopts some aspects of SCHOPENHAUER'S metaphysics in this book, distinguishing between a world of appearance and an underlying reality, as well as adopting Schopenhauer's bleak view of the human condition. But Nietzsche goes even farther than Schopenhauer in his valuation of art. For Schopenhauer, art provides a temporary respite from suffering. For Nietzsche, art can have a life-affirming effect.

Two central notions in *The Birth of Tragedy* are the Dionysian and the Apollonian; these are forces or drives that he names after the Greek deities. He uses these terms in discussing metaphysics, psychology, and in discussing art. The Apollonian is characterized by clarity, dream, self-control, and BEAUTY. Metaphysically speaking, the Apollonian is associated with Schopenhauer's "world of representation." The Dionysian is characterized by intoxication, loss of self, and the

SUBLIME (i.e., awe-inspiring and overpowering); metaphysically, the Dionysian is associated with Schopenhauer's Will.

Some art forms are predominantly Apollonian, such as sculpture, painting, and epic poetry; other art forms are predominantly Dionysian, such as music and dance. Still others are a more balanced combination of the two forces, such as Greek tragedy. Through the creation of art, these drives sublimate the despair of the human condition. Greek tragedy has its origins in the chorus component, which showed the Greek spectators the bleak truth about human life (the chorus is the Dionysian aspect of tragedy), while simultaneously making that truth bearable through the detached, aesthetic representation (this occurs insofar as the characters are present as if in a dream, an illusion; this is the Apollonian aspect). Retaining the Dionysian element is important; tragedy does not avoid facing the truths of human existence, as do more purely Apollonian arts, such as epic poetry. The third force Nietzsche considers in *The Birth of Tragedy* is the drive to theoretical understanding; Nietzsche locates this drive historically in the fifth century B.C.E., in Socrates' disruption of the traditional "archaic" Greek culture.

Not too long after *The Birth of Tragedy* (in *Human all too Human*), Nietzsche discards the Kantian notion that there is a distinction between the way the world seems and the way it really is; he drops the Schopenhauerian metaphysics. This later Nietzsche holds that the world of experience is all there is. This results in an adjustment of the previous claim regarding the value of art. Art no longer justifies the (real) world (there is no real, ultimate reality set apart from the world of experience). In this later period, the claim is that art makes our existence *bearable*; it does so by taking the edge off of the harsh truths of existence, by formulating small lies, by constructing beautiful illusions (to be contrasted with the big lies of religion). In his unpublished notes collected as *The Will to Power*, Nietzsche writes, "For a philosopher to say, 'the good and the beautiful are one', is infamy; if he goes on to add, 'also the true', one ought to thrash him. Truth is ugly. —We possess *art* lest we *perish of the truth.*" Art misrepresents only modestly, and so retains a "good intellectual conscience"; religion, however, tells bigger lies (also for the purpose of making life bearable), and so manifests "the bad intellectual conscience."

Nietzsche holds that we can employ this minimal misrepresentation technique to ourselves as well, "to 'give style' to one's character."

We do this by concealing certain parts of our character, emphasizing other parts, and creatively reinterpreting yet other parts. See METAPHOR.

Further Reading

Nehamas, A. (1985), *Nietzsche: Life as Literature,* Cambridge, MA: Harvard University Press.
Nietzsche, F. (1999 [1872]), *The Birth of Tragedy and Other Writings,* R. Geuss and R. Speirs (eds), R. Speirs (trans.). Cambridge: Cambridge University Press.
—(2001 [1882, 1887]), *The Gay Science,* B. Williams (ed.), J. Nauckhoff (trans.). Cambridge: Cambridge University Press.
Ridley, Aaron (2006), *Routledge Philosophy GuideBook to Nietzsche on Art.* London and New York: Routledge.
Young, J. (1992), *Nietzsche's Philosophy of Art.* Cambridge: Cambridge University Press.

Plato (428–348 B.C.E.)

Plato, Socrates' principal disciple, was born into an aristocratic family in Athens, Greece, where he founded his Academy, in 385 B.C.E. ARISTOTLE studied at Plato's Academy for 20 years, leaving only after Plato's death. Plato is the most important figure in the history of Western philosophy. Even this role was exaggerated in the famous remark made by the British philosopher Alfred North Whitehead (1861–1947): "The safest general characterization of the European philosophical tradition is that it consists of a series of footnotes to Plato" (1979, p. 39). The fact that philosophers recognize that there is some truth to this remark speaks to Plato's significance. Plato's writing systematically addresses a number of topics: ETHICS, POLITICS, metaphysics, and epistemology, to name only a few.

Plato put forward a theory of poetry, tragedy, painting, and so on, which evolved into the most enduring theory of art; according to Plato, artists imitate nature; this is the first theory of art as REPRESENTATION. But Plato is famously critical of the arts in the *Republic,* on metaphysical, epistemic, and moral grounds. Regarding the latter, as well as a worry about art's tendency to provoke the emotions, he formulates what has been an enduring argument in favor of CENSORSHIP, which is deeply woven into the psychological and political considerations of the book. See PLATO, REPUBLIC. Other Platonic dialogues relevant to the philosophy of art are the *Symposium*, *Phaedrus*, and *Ion*. See CREATIVITY, EMOTION, ETHICS, LITERATURE, and TRAGEDY.

Further Reading

Fine, G. (ed.) (2011), *The Oxford Handbook of Plato*. Oxford and New York: Oxford University Press.
Hamilton, E. and Cairns, H. (eds) (2005), *The Collected Dialogues of Plato*. Princeton, NJ: Princeton University Press.
Whitehead, A. N. (1979), *Process and Reality*. New York: The Free Press.

Schopenhauer, Arthur (1788–1860)

Schopenhauer was a transcendental idealist philosopher influenced by Immanuel KANT, and a major influence upon Friedrich NIETZSCHE. Regarding the Kantian influence, Schopenhauer draws a distinction between the way the world really is and the way it seems. The latter, the world of our everyday experience, is a world of appearance, an illusion, the phenomenal world; this is the world as representation, or Idea. The world in-itself, ultimate reality, is "Will," a nonrational, blind, impersonal, purposeless, power or urging (which is to some extent knowable, in contrast to Kant's *noumena*). The phenomenal world consists of objectifications or expressions of the will. Schopenhauer's view of human life is deeply pessimistic. At the core of our nature is striving, desiring; our desires are occasionally satisfied but new ones always arise. Human nature is characterized by suffering.

We can escape this unpleasant constant desiring by means of DISINTERESTED aesthetic experiences (see AESTHETIC EXPERIENCE); these experiences temporarily disengage the individual will by bracketing our interests and desires. Thus, the VALUE OF ART is central to Schopenhauer's view of human life. At the same time, art serves a cognitive function. Through the arts, we can come to know universals; Schopenhauer, in fact, holds that, through works of art, we can come to know PLATO's forms ("Ideas"). Through poetry for example, we apprehend *humanity,* not in relation to a particular person's actions, but humanity in general. All art forms, except music, copy the Ideas. (Note that ARISTOTLE believed that we can acquire general truths through poetry but Plato did not.) Schopenhauer reserves a special place for music. Whereas the other arts copy Ideas, music presents (is a copy of) ultimate reality, the Will (not the human will but the Will itself). Music, like the world of our experience, is an objectification or expression of the Will.

Further Reading

Alperson, P. (1981), "Schopenhauer and musical revelation." *Journal of Aesthetics and Art Criticism,* 40(2): 155–66.
Jacquette, D. (ed.) (1996), *Schopenhauer, Philosophy and the Arts.* Cambridge: Cambridge University Press.
Schopenhauer, A. (1966 [1819/44]), *The World as Will and Representation,* E. J. F. Payne (trans.). New York: Dover.

Sibley, Frank Noel (1923–96)

The British philosopher Frank Sibley maintains that there is a special faculty that enables those who possess it to perceive the AESTHETIC PROPERTIES that aesthetic concepts pick out; this is the faculty of taste. *Green, square,* and *curved* are examples of nonaesthetic concepts; *graceful, moving, powerful, tense, trite, garish, awkward,* and BEAUTIFUL are examples of aesthetic concepts. Aesthetic properties depend for their existence upon nonaesthetic properties; for example, the gracefulness of a painting depends upon some nonaesthetic features of the painting, perhaps its curved lines. However, although a particular aesthetic property may depend for its existence upon one or another nonaesthetic property, we cannot infer from nonaesthetic properties to the existence of particular aesthetic properties. To put this another way, aesthetic properties are not positively condition-governed. Aesthetic properties are emergent properties; perceivers with taste see them straightaway. Sibley does allow that we may be able to reason about which aesthetic properties a work does *not* have, based on its nonaesthetic properties. Perhaps, for example, we can argue that a painting with only square shapes will not be graceful. Many philosophers have subsequently taken issue with Sibley's claims, including the very distinction between aesthetic and nonaesthetic properties (notably, Ted Cohen, Peter Kivy, Roger Scruton, and Marcia Eaton). Sibley's seminal paper is "Aesthetic Concepts" (1959).

Further Reading

Brady, E. and Levinson, J. (eds) (2001), *Aesthetic Concepts: Essays after Sibley.* Oxford: Clarendon Press.
Sibley, F. (1959), "Aesthetic concepts." *Philosophical Review*, 68, 42: 1–50.
—(1965), "Aesthetic and Non-Aesthetic." *Philosophical Review*, 74: 135–59.

Walton, Kendall (b. 1939)

Walton's influential view of artistic REPRESENTATION is that it is a kind of game of make-believe in which paintings, novels, and films are props that prescribe what we are to imagine. A painting represents a chocolate soufflé, say, if it guides us, prompts us to imagine that we are seeing a soufflé. (Walton suggests that the prop and imagining aspects of his account explain Richard WOLLHEIM'S "twofoldness" of seeing-in.)

Unlike paintings, photographs are transparent in the sense that we really see what is pictured through them, somewhat like we see people through a window or objects through a telescope. In paintings, we do not directly see the objects depicted; painters' beliefs affect the rendering of the depicted objects. Photography is a mechanical medium in that this mediation is absent; the relation between a photograph's subject matter and a photograph is causal.

It seems odd that readers often react EMOTIONALLY to characters and situations in fiction. It seems odd to feel pity, say, for an unreal person. Isn't it a reasonable presupposition that we can only really feel pity for people whom we believe to be real? (This line of thought assumes a cognitivist theory of the emotions.) This is known as the "paradox of fiction." Following his general theory of representation, Walton proposes that the requisite beliefs are make-beliefs, beliefs about fictional characters in a novel, for instance. The emotions we feel are real, but they are real only within the game; pity for a character in a novel, for instance, is "quasi-pity."

The AESTHETIC PROPERTIES one perceives a work to have do not depend merely upon a work's nonaesthetic properties (see SIBLEY). Aesthetic properties depend also upon the art *category* to which one takes the work to belong. That is, if I perceive a work as belonging to one category, I may perceive some aesthetic properties that I would not perceive were I to take it to belong to another. The categorization of works of art is not a relative matter; works of art really do belong to certain categories. Categorizations are settled in part by considering a work's origin, the artist's intentions, and the art-historical context. See FILM, LITERATURE.

Further Reading

Walton, K. (1970), "Categories of art." *Philosophical Review*, 79, 334–67.
—(1990), *Mimesis as Make-Believe*. Cambridge, MA: Harvard University Press.

Wollheim, Richard (1923–2003)

Richard Wollheim was a British philosopher who wrote on a range of issues in the philosophy of art. Regarding ONTOLOGY, he maintains that works of art are not a unified category. Some works of art, such as paintings and sculptures, are physical objects; works of music, novels, and so on, are types, and instances of these works (a particular copy of a given novel, for example) are tokens. He contrasts types with universals and classes, arguing that the relation between types and tokens is closer than the relation between the others and their elements (see his 1980).

Wollheim's most enduringly influential contribution concerns pictorial REPRESENTATION, that is, depiction. According to Wollheim, pictorial representation rests on our natural human capacity to see one thing in another (a variation on Ludwig Wittgenstein's "seeing-as"). For example, it is possible to see an animal in a cloud or the

Virgin Mary in a pizza. Seeing a picture as depicting something is an experience Wollheim calls "seeing-in." What we see in a painting is just what is represented. Moreover, we see not only what is depicted but are simultaneously aware of the painting's surface features (brush strokes, and so on). The experience possesses what Wollheim calls "twofoldness," twofold seeing. Seeing-in occurs even when there is no representation. One can see an animal in a cloud, but this is not depiction; depiction requires there being some sense to being right or wrong about what you see-in, and for Wollheim, this is a matter of the artist's intentions. (See WALTON, VISUAL ART.)

Further Reading

Hopkins, A., Savile, A. (eds) (1992), *Psychoanalisis, Mind, and Art: Perspectives on Richard Wollheim*. Oxford: Blackwell.
Wollheim, R. (1973), *On Art and the Mind: Essays and Lectures*. London: Allen Lane.
—(1980), *Art and Its Objects: An Introduction to Aesthetics* (2nd edn). Cambridge: Cambridge University Press.
—(1987), *Painting as an Art*. Princeton, NJ: Princeton University Press.

Key Texts

Aristotle, *Poetics* (circa 335 B.C.E.)

Aristotle's principal work in philosophy of art is the *Poetics*. The *Poetics* was not written for the public, but like most of Aristotle's surviving work, it consists of lecture notes. The primary focus of the text is a detailed analysis of one particular genre of poetry, tragedy (part two of the *Poetics*, which is lost, focused on comedy). Aristotle categorizes poetry, painting, sculpture, dance, and music as *technai* (the plural of "*technē*," which is often translated as "art"). More specifically, a *technē* is any skillful activity based on principles, including activities such as carpentry and medicine, which, of course, we now take to be quite different from the fine arts. Poetry, painting, et cetera, are distinguished from other *technai* insofar as they are instances of imitation (*mimēsis*); imitation is a necessary condition of these arts (see REPRESENTATION). Aristotle points out that we naturally find imitations pleasurable; this is one source of the pleasure we experience through art. Each art is demarcated in terms of its medium (the materials), its subject matter, and the manner or point of view of the imitation (the method). For example, tragedy uses language, harmony, and rhythm to represent the actions of serious, superior, admirable people (as opposed to comedy, which imitates the actions of inferior people). Unlike epic poetry (Homer, for instance), in tragedy, the story is told through the characters rather than a narrator.

Aristotle claims that tragedy has a therapeutic effect on spectators; the spectators undergo a catharsis, which, according to the traditional interpretation, is a kind of purging (also see book VIII of Aristotle's *Politics*). EMOTIONS such as fear and pity can be aroused in the spectators of a tragedy; such experiences purge or vent these emotions (and perhaps similar, destructive emotions), which otherwise may be disruptive. This is the purpose (*telos*) of tragedy. An alternate interpretation construes the arousal of pity and fear to be educative. According to this interpretation, catharsis is a kind of clarification; through the experience of a tragedy, a spectator *calibrates* her emotions; she learns when it is appropriate to experience an emotion such as pity, to what degree, and so on. Either way, tragedy contributes to our psychological well-being.

In characterizing tragedy, Aristotle emphasizes plot. A BEAUTIFUL, or artistically excellent, tragedy is plot-driven and represents a complete action; it has a beginning, middle, and an end, in which the events unfold in a believable manner, and it focuses on the general types of characters, actions, and events rather than particular cases. It is reasonable to take a plot to be an arrangement of events; since a work's form is the arrangement of its elements (whether these are musical notes or the lines, colors, and shapes of a painting), some have interpreted Aristotle's view as an early example of FORMALISM.

Aristotle's account yields a defense of poetry against Plato's critique (see PLATO, REPUBLIC). Aristotle agreed with Plato that poetry arouses the emotions, but as we have seen, poetry does not merely strengthen the emotions, endangering the authority of our reason; rather, poetry brings about a catharsis. Moreover, in another contrast to Plato, Aristotle maintains that we not only derive pleasure from poetry's *mimesis* and catharsis, but we can learn from poetry; through its depiction of specific characters and their actions, poetry can convey general truths about human affairs—this is more like philosophical knowledge (having to do with general truths) than it is like the truths in history, which have to do with particulars.

Further Reading

Aristotle (1984). *Rhetoric*, W. R. Roberts (trans.). New York: Random House.
—(1986), *The Poetics of Aristotle*, S. Halliwell (trans.). London: Duckworth.
Belfiore, E. S. (1992), *Tragic Pleasures: Aristotle on Plot and Emotion*. Princeton, NJ: Princeton University Press.
Rorty, A. (ed.) (1992), *Essays on Aristotle's Poetics*. Princeton, NJ: Princeton University Press.

Bell, Clive, *Art* (1914)

Bell focuses upon the formal elements of visual art, which include the relations among lines, colors, shapes, and so on. He argues that some visual artifacts possess a special sort of design, which he calls *significant form*. It is in virtue of possessing this special form that an artifact attains art status. Significant form is the essential quality of visual works of art. He writes, "For either all works of visual art have some common quality, or when we speak of 'works of art' we gibber" (Chapter 1). How do we know that an artifact possesses significant form? We know because such artifacts arouse a particular *kind* of emotion, which Bell calls the *aesthetic emotion*. The aesthetic emotion is something like an AESTHETIC EXPERIENCE, more profound than standard emotions such as sadness (different works of art elicit different aesthetic emotions but these emotions are of the same kind). Bell's influence stretches beyond considerations of visual art.

Bell pits his formalism primarily against an understanding of art based on its subject matter, REPRESENTATIONAL content. He claims not only that a work's representational elements are not the principal ingredient of art but that representational elements are *irrelevant* to an artifact's art status and value. The only way in which the content may be relevant is in virtue of its form. Bell is also critical of representational elements insofar as they may distract a viewer from noticing a work of art's form. This position on content has been widely criticized; one problem with the claim that representational elements are irrelevant is that we often need to engage with these elements in order to properly grasp a work of art's form. Nöel Carroll offers an example that effectively demonstrates this point: Pieter Bruegel's *Landscape with the Fall of Icarus* (1558). In the painting, we only see Icarus's leg; it is very small, flailing in the water in the lower, right corner of the painting. If a viewer does not grasp that this painting is, in one sense or another, about Icarus, the form will appear very different than it does when one is aware that *that* is Icarus's leg. Thus it appears that, in some cases at least, correctly apprehending content is crucial even to perceiving form correctly (see pp. 123–5 of Carroll's 1999).

Even though Bell takes significant form to be the essential quality of art, his emphasis on the aesthetic emotion makes his view a sort of impure formalism; his view is based ultimately upon our subjective engagement with art. This can be contrasted with Eduard Hanslick's (1825–1904) purer, musical FORMALISM. Bell has also been widely criticized for not clarifying what significant form is, for not giving principles of significant form. It is not enough to say that significant form is the kind of form that stirs the aesthetic emotion; we need a way of understanding what significant form is, independently of its giving rise to the aesthetic emotion. In other words, what exactly is it about the structure of certain works of art that makes their form significant? Bell offers examples of great works that are supposed to possess significant form but this seems inadequate; he mentions artists and works such as the paintings of Paul Cézanne (1839–1906); the frescoes of Giotto di Bondone (1267–1337); the stained glass windows at Chartres Cathedral, France; and the St. Sophia Church (Kiev, Ukraine). Bell is also criticized for not clarifying the aesthetic emotion. Philosophers wish that Bell had attempted to elucidate each of these key concepts independently; instead, he conceives of each as evidence for the other. Another short-coming of Bell's view is that it leaves no room for bad art; a painting, for instance, which lacks significant form is not bad art; rather, it is just not art at all. See DEFINITIONS OF ART.

Further Reading

Bell, C. (1987 [1914]), *Art* (3rd edn). Oxford: Oxford University Press.
—(1922), *Since Cézanne*. London: Chatto & Windus.
Carroll, N. (1989), "Clive Bell's aesthetic hypothesis," in G. Dickie, R. Sclafani, and R. Roblin (eds), *Aesthetics: A Critical Anthology* (2nd edn). New York: St. Martin's Press, pp. 84–95.
Carroll, N. (1999), *Philosophy of Art: A Contemporary Introduction*. London and New York: Routledge Press.
Dickie, G. T. (1965), "Clive Bell and the method of *Principia Ethica*." *British Journal of Aesthetics*, 5: 139–43.

Collingwood, R. G., *Principles of Art* (1938)

Collingwood's text is known primarily for his expression theory of art, his idealist ontology, and his distinction between art and craft. Regarding the latter, according to Collingwood, skill, technique is not a necessary feature of artistic activity; these typically focus on bringing about preconceived ends, such as the arousal of emotion; conceived in these terms, art would be a means to some end (as would its being valued for bringing about pleasure, amusement, or the pictorial representation of an object). He contrasts such craft—what he calls "the technical theory of art"—with "art proper." Regarding art proper, artists do not work with a preconceived end in mind. Works of art may involve the use of technique, of course, but this is neither a necessary nor sufficient condition for art status.

Although he espouses an expression theory, he maintains that the creative process does not begin with a fully formed emotion (as it does on Tolstoy's view; see EMOTION). Rather, the artistic process begins with an inchoate emotion, a "perturbation or excitement," which spurs the artist to work. Through the creative process of imaginative expression, guided by this germ of an emotion, the work clarifies the emotion, renders it intelligible. The emotion only becomes conscious in expression. Notice that this notion of expression is very different from the sort of venting of emotion accomplished through crying or throwing a temper tantrum; in such cases, there is no clarification. This clarificatory expression is necessary and sufficient for art status; art is defined as an activity. What is more, for Collingwood, this is a process of self-discovery.

In emphasizing artists' creative activity, Collingwood de-emphasizes the physical objects often considered to be works of art, such as the painted canvas, chiseled sculpture, written or spoken poem, and sounds of music. Collingwood's philosophy of art rests on a controversial, idealist ONTOLOGY. He holds that a painting, for instance, is not to be identified with the painted canvas; a painting is a mental object. A poem or a tune may exist even though it has never been written, spoken, or hummed. It exists in the artist's head. This mental object is the creative product, the work of art; the painted canvas is not. More accurately, the work of art is not a thing but an activity; the work of art is the "total imaginative experience."

Although works of art can exist without any physical manifestation, physical objects are important for art in the sense that, through her interaction with it, the artist develops complexities of experience that she could not develop without it. Moreover, the physical object makes the work of art available for spectators. Through sufficiently imaginative engagement with the painted canvas, for example, a spectator can seek an experience that is identical with that of the artist; the spectator imaginatively reconstructs the mental work of art.

In arguing for this ontological position, Collingwood makes some reasonable observations that are reminiscent of Roman Ingarden's observations (see PHENOMENOLOGY). For example, there are many features of a given work of art that are not features of the painted canvas, which require active aesthetic experience, such as represented objects, the depiction of space, and so on. Just as we need to reconstruct a speaker's meaning while listening to a lecture, works of art require imaginative reconstruction. And vice versa, there are features of the painted canvas that are not features of the work of art, such as its weight, scuffs on the back, and so on. Moreover, Collingwood's idea that the audience must imaginatively recreate the work of art is akin to Ingarden's notion of "concretization." Collingwood's ontology has some unwelcome consequences, such as that works of art go in and out of existence as the requisite mental states exist or do not. Finally, it bears mentioning that in *The Principles of Art*, Collingwood draws upon and refines a number of claims made by Benedetto Croce (1866–1952), so much so that the expression theory discussed above is often referred to as the "Croce–Collingwood" view.

Further Reading

Collingwood, R. G. (1958), *The Principles of Art*. New York: Oxford University Press.
Croce, B. (1965), *Guide to Aesthetics*, P. Romanell (trans.). New York: Bobbs-Merrill.
Kemp, G. (2003), "The Croce-Collingwood theory as theory." *Journal of Aesthetics and Art Criticism*, 61: 171–93.
Neill, A. (1998), *R. G. Collingwood: A Philosophy of Art*. London: Orion Books.

Danto, *The Transfiguration of the Commonplace* (see Danto, Arthur in Key Thinkers)

Dewey, John, *Art as Experience* (1934)

Dewey laments the typical separation of art from life, which he believes stands in the way of effective theorizing about art. To understand art, we cannot simply examine the objects we find on display in an art gallery, which are compartmentalized in this way not as a result of their nature but due to the forces of imperialism, nationalism, capitalism, and so on. Dewey emphasizes that understanding art requires us to rediscover the connections between art and everyday life. This requires an examination, first, of everyday experiences, and next, an examination of *heightened* everyday experiences, which Dewey takes to be aesthetic experiences in germ.

Dewey's naturalism is on display as he grounds the aesthetic in the most basic aspects of human life, and on the degree to which we are intertwined with our environment (note that this aspect of his view resonates with the position of existential PHENOMENOLOGISTS). When we fall out of balance with our environment, we experience it (undergo it) as a lack, a tension. We then act in order to regain equilibrium. In these qualities of ordinary experience lie the bases of the aesthetic: the phases of undergoing and doing are the bases of tension and rhythm in art; reaching equilibrium is the basis of order, form, and harmony.

Dewey distinguishes between two kinds of normal experiences. Run-of-the-mill experiences are inchoate, they are cut off; they dissipate before reaching fulfillment. *"An experience"* (a.k.a. an "integral experience"), in contrast, is unified, possesses a pervasive quality, which Dewey calls aesthetic; it is a complete experience; that is, it continues until it reaches a consummation. Such experiences stand out, for example, *"that* storm," *"that* meal," *"that* conversation."* An example of the latter may be a significant talk with a friend, which involves tensions, resolutions, high points, low points, but which ultimately concludes in a way that unifies every element into a single experience.

Although *"an* experience" possesses an aesthetic quality, this does not mean that every such experience is an aesthetic experience. What sets aesthetic experiences apart from integral experiences that are not aesthetic experiences is that, in aesthetic experiences, the unity is achieved by means of a single pervasive, aesthetic quality *which has been developed and accentuated.* According to Dewey, we can have aesthetic experiences of things outside the domain of art; we can have aesthetic experiences of NATURE, scientific hypotheses, and so on. Notice that Dewey's account of aesthetic experience does not rely on a notion of DISINTEREST or an aesthetic attitude; rather, he emphasizes the *connections* between the aesthetic and the practical, the every day. This feature of his account resonates with continental philosophers and puts him at odds with Monroe BEARDSLEY'S account of aesthetic experience.

Art *products*, such as paintings and statues, are not to be identified with "the work of art"; the work of art *is* experience, in the sense that it is through aesthetic experiences that artists create art products, and it is by engaging with these products that spectators reconstruct similar aesthetic experiences. While the fine arts are useful products for generating aesthetic experiences, as we have seen, other kinds of products are as well; POPULAR ART, for example, may be just as productive of aesthetic experience as fine art. While Dewey agrees with FORMALISTS that the formal features of works of art are salient regarding aesthetic experience, he understands form to be dynamic, and does not agree that the formal features are experienced as disconnected from other aspects of our lives: "The habitual properties of lines cannot be got rid of even in an experiment that endeavors to isolate the experience of lines from everything else. The properties of objects that lines define and of movements they relate are too deeply embedded" (1980, p. 101)

Dewey's view of artistic EXPRESSION resembles R. G. COLLINGWOOD'S in some respects. For example, Dewey maintains, with Collingwood, that a mere venting of emotions does not amount to expression; in addition, an artist does not know what she will express in advance; expression involves clarifying an initial "impulsion" or mood through an art form's medium, guided by a pervasive quality. One way in which Dewey's view of expression differs from traditional views of expression is that, for Dewey, what gets expressed is not simply the mental state of the artist; in fact, Dewey's view of EMOTION in general resembles that of an existential phenomenologist rather than an Anglo-American philosopher. Another difference from Collingwood's view is ONTOLOGICAL; Dewey's theory of art is not idealist; Collingwood's theory is. For Dewey, clarifying the initial impulsion in the art form's *material* is crucial, as is the intention to communicate.

Further Reading

Carroll, N. (2001), "Four concepts of aesthetic experience," in his *Beyond Aesthetics: Philosophical Essays*. Cambridge: Cambridge University Press.

Dewey, J. (1980 [1934]), *Art as Experience*. New York: Perigee.

Leddy, T. (2011) "Dewey's aesthetics," in E. Zalta (ed.), *The Stanford Encyclopedia of Philosophy.* http://plato.stanford.edu/entries/dewey-aesthetics

Shusterman, R. (1992), *Pragmatist Aesthetics: Living Beauty, Rethinking Art.* Oxford: Blackwell.

Goodman, *Languages of Art* (see Goodman, Nelson in Key Thinkers)

Hegel, G. W. F., *Lectures on Fine Art* (1835)

Unlike many of his predecessors, Hegel is not focused on AESTHETIC JUDGMENTS or the AESTHETIC EXPERIENCES of individuals. Broadly speaking, he is focused on the VALUE OF ART. What is particularly noteworthy about Hegel's approach is that he focuses on the meaning and value of art at the cultural level, rather than at the level of the individual. At their best, works of art can express a culture's worldview, its ethos; art can express "the deepest interests of mankind, and the most comprehensive truths of the spirit . . . . the *Divine*" (1975, Vol. I, p. 7). Art that accomplishes this is BEAUTIFUL; unlike Immanuel KANT, Hegel understands beauty to be a property of works of art, not a function of their effects. Famously, Hegel emphasizes history. History does not proceed arbitrarily; rather, history unfolds rationally, aiming toward a goal; the goal is individual human freedom; as worldviews change from epoch to epoch, so does art's subject matter.

Consider three notions of spirit (*Geist*): "subjective spirit" refers to individual psychology; "objective spirit" refers to the common spirit of a community, manifest in social institutions. Art, religion, and philosophy are all forms of "absolute spirit," which consists of spirit going beyond the individual and the finitely social to become self-conscious. Art, religion, and philosophy not only aid in spirit's self-understanding (spirit becomes self-conscious through expression), they also *convey* spirit's understanding of itself (this is the worldview). Art, religion, and philosophy do this in different ways. Art expresses perceptually (in paint, words, sounds, and so on). Religion employs mental imagery. Philosophy employs conceptual thought. In each historical period, one of these forms of absolute spirit is most effective in conveying the epoch's ethos.

Hegel describes three styles or phases of art: the symbolic, the classical, and the romantic. Art surpasses religion and philosophy as the most effective means of cultural expression in the classical phase. In each phase, one art form is most effective; Hegel focuses on poetry, music, painting, architecture, and sculpture. Examples of symbolic art are Egyptian monuments. Symbolic art fails to adequately express its content due to the vagueness and indeterminacy of the content itself, namely, the mythological and religious themes that constitute the worldviews of the relevant cultures. The dominant art form of this phase is architecture, the most material, physical of the arts. Even Egyptian monuments do not precisely embody the Egyptian spirit but rather only point to it (symbolize it). Architecture cannot adequately express the more complex content of future periods.

Art is the principal means of cultural expression in the classical phase of art, which is the historical period of classical Greece. In this phase, art's perceptual means of expression align perfectly with the Greek worldview, represented in the free individuality of the Greek gods. The dominant art form in this phase is sculpture, which succeeds in embodying this content insofar as its medium enables it to express more complex content than architecture. This classical perceptual embodiment of the freedom of spirit is what Hegel calls "true" or "ideal" beauty.

The final phase of art, romantic art, occurs in the Christian period. The content is *inwardness*; the freedom is one of human subjectivity. Art that expresses this content achieves "spiritual beauty." The arts that excel in expressing this content are able to embody more complexities by engaging the imagination, by being less dependent upon the material aspect of the work, and by being more intimate. Painting is effective; music more so; poetry is the most effective art in this phase, due to its conceptual capacities. Artistic expression, in general, reaches its peak and limit with poetry. According to Hegel, during this period, art had exhausted its potential (having peaked in the classical phase). The ethos of the culture of Hegel's time was best conveyed through religion and philosophy. It is in this sense that art had come to an end. See DANTO on the end of art. Also see MARXISM, NATURE, and VALUE OF ART.

Further Reading

Hegel, G. W. F. (1975 [1835]), *Lectures on Fine Art*, T. M. Knox (trans.). Oxford: Clarendon Press.
Houlgate, St. (ed.) (2007), *Hegel and the Arts*. Evanston, IL: Northwestern University Press.
Wicks, R. (1993), "Hegel's aesthetics: An overview," in F. C. Beiser (ed.), *The Cambridge Companion to Hegel*. Cambridge: Cambridge University Press.

Heidegger, Martin, "The Origin of the Work of Art" (1936)

According to Heidegger, works of art are not to be understood as physical things; their essence is not imitation (see REPRESENTATION); works of art are also not understandable simply as objects with special, AESTHETIC PROPERTIES. Rather, works of art have two essential traits: a work of art sets up, or gathers together, a world, and it sets forth the earth. A reader new to Heidegger will wonder about the meaning of "world" and "earth"; clearly, Heidegger is not using these terms in an ordinary fashion. Regarding a world, Heidegger considers a painting of a peasant woman's shoes by Van Gogh; he claims that this painting does not merely represent those shoes; rather, the painting gathers together the world of the peasant woman.

For Heidegger, a world is not the earth, universe, or some other place; rather, a world is a context that enables us to make sense of things. The world is a cluster of background practices, equipment, skills, and so on that render things intelligible. Consider these examples of more limited and narrow cases of worlds (these are not Heidegger's examples): the medical world and the drug culture (world). The same physical object can have a different meaning in each world; take, for example, a syringe. The medical world provides a context in which a syringe has the function of a piece of equipment used for treating patients with the aim of improving health. The drug world provides a context in which the syringe has the function of injecting heroin with the aim of getting high. Note that each world has norms and values that are grounded on the world's background practices.

In a larger sense of world, at the scope of an epoch, Heidegger claims that the best works of art provide the background context on the basis of which anything makes sense to begin with; the work of art establishes a kind of cultural paradigm. A Greek temple, for example, creates a background against which events and phenomena come to have the meaning they do for that culture. "It is the temple work that first structures and simultaneously gathers around itself the unity of those paths and relations in which birth and death, disaster and blessing, victory and disgrace, endurance and decline acquire for the human being the shape of its destiny" (2002, pp. 20–1).

In order to give the reader some leverage for understanding this basic idea, notice that there is something very similar, albeit much more limited, that we often say about works of art. Consider the film *Elizabethtown* (2005). In the film, a young man's father dies, right at the time the young man's professional life has completely collapsed. The protagonist returns to his father's hometown for the services and burial. He engages with long-lost, extended family members, and rediscovers who his father was through these relationships. Groundwork is being laid for the young man to remake his understanding of life in general, his father, and himself. He meets someone, a romantic interest. She realizes that he needs to think long and hard about his family, his life, and about how to move forward. For his long drive home, she burns for him a set of mixed CDs that are coordinated with a homemade, illustrated map of his journey home; the map includes instructions about where to stop, what to see, and what to do. The point I am trying to make is small in scope (there are certainly deeper points to make about the film): *Elizabethtown* generates a new way of conceiving of a long drive; the work of art makes it possible for long drives to be intelligible in a new way. A long drive—understood as a vehicle for rebuilding one's understanding of oneself—is made possible in the light of the film. Although similar in terms of creating a new way to make sense of something, the Greek temple does much more than this, of course, it opens up, it sets up, a world, in the sense that it *unifies* what everything means for that culture. It sets up norms, standards, and background practices.

The second essential trait of works of art is that they set forth the earth. Heidegger uses "earth" as a metaphor to refer to those aspects of works of art that grab our attention but which also remain hidden, indeterminate, in the background. Consider these examples of such elements: a temple stone's texture, *particular* colors in a painting, *particular* pitches and rhythms in music (not merely aqua but that particular, slightly dark aqua; not merely an eighth-note, but that particular, slightly early eighth-note). If we attempt a scientific analysis of these properties, we can, indeed, specify them, but in doing so, their original effects disappear. When such properties are *working*, their specificity is hidden. As Heidegger writes, "Color shines and wants only to shine. If we try to make it comprehensible by analyzing it into numbers of oscillations it is gone" (2002, p. 25).

Two additional, important issues raised in Heidegger's essay have to do with strife and truth. In works of art, earth and world are set in a kind of competition with each other; they are in strife. This strife doesn't curb the effects of each but rather enables each to excel in its own domain. Through this strife between earth and world, truth happens. The traditional notion of truth is that truth is correspondence; truth is the correspondence between (say) our statements and reality. Heidegger maintains that prior to any such correspondence—in order for us to be able to check to determine whether there is correspondence—reality, the facts, must be *unconcealed*. Truth, for Heidegger, is unconcealment. One of the ways in which unconcealment occurs is through a work of art. This is not a reference to imitation; the idea is not that truth happens in a work of art when that which is REPRESENTED is represented accurately. "Being," for Heidegger, is, roughly, that on the basis of which things are intelligible (according to one interpretation). Unconcealment in art is a creation of being. Great art is something on the basis of which events, phenomena, and people become intelligible in new ways. The best works of art enable us to make sense of things in a new way. See CREATIVITY; PHENOMENOLOGY.

Further Reading

Heidegger, M. (2002 [1936]), "The origin of the work of art," in J. Young and K. Haynes (eds), *Off the Beaten Track*. Cambridge: Cambridge University Press.

Kockelmans, J. (1985), *Heidegger on Art and Art Works*. Dordrecht: Nijhoff.

Young, J. (2001), *Heidegger's Philosophy of Art*. Cambridge: Cambridge University Press.

Hume, David, "Of the Standard of Taste" (1757)

The ideas put forward in Hume's essay were influenced by, and in some cases, simply borrowed from Joseph Addison, Francis Hutcheson (see BEAUTY), Anthony Ashley Cooper (Earl of Shaftesbury), and Abbé Jean-Baptiste Du Bos. The essay is an important precursor to Immanuel Kant's treatment of aesthetic judgment in his CRITIQUE OF JUDGMENT (1790), but it is not known if Kant read Hume's essay. In "Of the Standard of Taste," Hume focuses on examples of literature.

For Hume, beauty is not a property of objects. If it were a property of objects, then we could straightforwardly determine the truth or falsity of a judgment that an object is beautiful: if I judge a work of art to be beautiful, and if beauty is, indeed, one of its properties, then the judgment is true. But Hume, following his predecessors, holds that beauty is a power certain objects possess to produce an agreeable sentiment (emotion), a certain kind of pleasure, a feeling of delight. In other words, I call an object beautiful because it possesses a power to produce pleasure in me when I perceive it, and I expect it will be pleasing to others. Hume does not give an account of the properties such objects have, as Hutcheson does (see BEAUTY); the focus is on the sentiment. (That said, there are writings in which Hume seems to emphasize an object's FORMAL properties, in virtue of which, it possesses the power to produce pleasure; also in contrast to Hutcheson, Hume believes that reason is involved; for more, see Hume's *A Treatise of Human Nature*.)

On the one hand, it does seem that aesthetic tastes differ to a large extent, especially when we consider the tastes of different cultures and in different periods of history. But, on the other hand, Hume observes that people in many different times and cultures seem to be in agreement about certain works of art that stand out and survive the test of time, such as the works of Homer and Virgil. At one point in the essay, Hume seems to maintain that there are certain aesthetic rules or principles that could provide guidelines for making and judging beautiful works of literature, and so on; these rules could be extracted from great works of art, established models. He does not give us effective examples of these principles, and he is unclear about exactly what their role is. Insofar as these would be cashed out in terms of qualities of objects, this is not his view.

The puzzle Hume confronts is that AESTHETIC JUDGMENTS are based on subjective experiences of pleasure, tastes vary widely (between cultures and times), yet these judgments are put forward as stronger than mere subjective opinions or preferences. He sets out to identify a standard of taste that will enable us to maintain that some judgments are better than others, even if judgments of taste are not the sort of judgments that can be true or false. In the end, Hume's view turns on the ideal critics he refers to as "true judges." He suggests that we can test judges vis-à-vis their views on aesthetic principles drawn from enduring works. But more importantly, his suggestion is that we can identify good judges, good critics, by examining *their* qualities: "Strong sense, united to delicate sentiment, improved by practice, perfected by comparison, and cleared of all prejudice" (Hume 1985, p. 247). And finally, "the *joint verdict* of such [judges], wherever they are to be found, is the true standard of taste and beauty" (Ibid., emphasis added). Some scholars detect a problem in the final portion of Hume's essay. Hume claims that even true judges will have irresolvable differences of taste; these differences are due to cultural differences and differences in temperament, based on a judge's age. See BEAUTY, AESTHETIC PROPERTIES, and TRAGEDY.

Further Reading

Carroll, N. (1984), "Hume's Standard of Taste." *Journal of Aesthetics and Art Criticism*, 43: 181–94.

Hume, D. (1985 [1757]), "Of the Standard of Taste," in E. Miller (ed.), *Essays Moral, Political, and Literary*. Indianapolis: Liberty Fund.

—(2000 [1739]), *A Treatise of Human Nature*, D. F. Norton and M. J. Norton (eds). Oxford: Oxford University Press.

Townsend, D. (2001), *Hume's Aesthetic Theory: Taste and Sentiment*. London: Routledge.

Kant, Immanuel, *Critique of Judgment* (1790)

Kant's third *Critique* is thought by many to be the foundational text of modern aesthetics. Kant addresses many important issues in this book; this entry deals only with the parts of the book that have been the most influential in the philosophy of art; namely, issues centering on Kant's account of judgments of taste, a.k.a. AESTHETIC JUDGMENTS. This portion of the book is a response to DAVID HUME'S "OF THE STANDARD OF TASTE" (although Kant does not explicitly engage with Hume's essay).

A judgment that a particular object is beautiful is a judgment of taste; for example, "This rose is beautiful," and "This painting is beautiful." Like Hume, Kant maintains that we cannot define BEAUTY in terms of (nor ground a judgment of taste on) qualities of objects, such as proportion, order, balance, and so on. There are simply no principles of beauty. In contrast to Hume, Kant maintains that a judgment of taste cannot be based on the testimony of experts. But we do, to be sure, find objects to be beautiful. If we cash this out only in terms of our approving *reaction* to an object, beauty will turn out to be nothing but a subjective preference; that is not the conclusion Kant wants to reach.

Kant holds that judgments of taste are grounded in subjective experiences of pleasure; that is, when we judge that something is beautiful, we do so because we experience pleasure. The pleasure at issue is not just any kind of pleasure but the kind of pleasure that arises from an experience that is occupied with an object *for its own sake*, namely, DISINTERESTED pleasure. This does not mean that such experiences are *un*-interested; being *dis*interested means that one is not interested in the object's existence nor in possessing it, or at least, that the pleasure at issue does not arise from this interest. This distinguishes pleasure in the beautiful from the gratifying (e.g., a sweet-tasting food), the practical, and the moral. In addition, we recognize that this is not merely a subjective preference, but we expect that others will find the object beautiful as well (even though there is no conceptual justification for this expectation); we hold that others *should* find the object to be beautiful. Finally, the pleasure in the object is due to the object's FORM; we experience the object as exhibiting order but not directed toward a purpose; the object has "merely formal purposiveness," or "purposiveness without purpose" (the purposiveness it does have has to do with the efficacy of its form).

The way we conceive of judgments of taste suggests that they are more than preferences. When we maintain that an object is beautiful, we intend for that judgment to carry more weight than stating a mere personal opinion, such as that pineapple pizza tastes good. According to Kant, we would not use the term "beautiful," if our intention were to express a mere personal preference. Disinterest provides another reason to think that these judgments are not merely subjective; the perceptual approach of disinterest seems to eliminate the partiality and idiosyncrasy involved in opinions based on the interested pleasures of sensuous gratification. The expected universal agreement of judgments of taste is ultimately due to the similarity of our mental faculties; this is why we expect, *a priori* (prior to experience), that everyone will experience the pleasure at issue. The relevant mental faculties are the imagination (which presents sensory information to the mind) and the understanding (which conceptually organizes sensory information). Kant claims that certain natural objects and artifacts spur these faculties into a kind of harmony or free-play—and since these faculties are common to everyone, everyone's faculties will undergo this harmony when presented with certain objects, which is experienced as pleasure. Thus, judgments of taste are based on subjective experiences of pleasure, but since the ground of this pleasure is common to us all, judgments of taste are not merely subjective. (See SUBLIME.)

Kant's discussion of beauty is primarily about natural objects. He takes beautiful objects in nature to provide examples of *free* beauty, and associated judgments to be *pure;* representational works of art provide examples of *dependent* beauty; associated judgments are *impure.* The latter are impure insofar as the judging involves taking the relevant concepts, purposes, and functions into consideration. (Instrumental music and perhaps abstract art fall into the category of free beauty.)

Creating art requires an innate capacity Kant calls genius, which provides the material for art (viz., "aesthetic ideas"), which enables an artist to be original, to do more than merely follow the rules of a given art form. In this sense, the work of artists is inexplicable; it cannot be conceptualized. But artists must also cultivate the skills to critically develop an original idea according to the standards of taste. Only by means of both genius and the cultivation of talent does a work of art become beautiful. See AESTHETIC EXPERIENCE; AESTHETIC PROPERTIES; CREATIVITY; NATURE; POPULAR ART; VALUE OF ART; ARCHITECTURE; BOURDIEU.

Further Reading

Cohen, T. and Guyer, P. (eds) (1982), *Essays in Kant's Aesthetics*. Chicago: University of Chicago Press.

Kant, I. (1987 [1790]). *Critique of Judgment*, W. Pluhar (trans.).
   Indianapolis: Hackett.
Kemal, S. (1993), *Kant's Aesthetic Theory*. New York: St Martin's Press.

Plato, *The Republic* (circa 360 B.C.E.)

The Republic is written as a dialogue in which Plato's conclusions
are typically expressed by the Socrates character. The main aim of
the book is to arrive at an account of justice; claims are made about
both individual and civic justice. Plato argues that imitative art is
harmful regarding both kinds of justice (imitative art represents its
subject matter by resembling it; see REPRESENTATION). The characters
in *The Republic* design an imaginary, perfectly just city, and conclude
that imitative art should be banned from that city.

Before looking at the reasoning behind these claims, it is important
to emphasize that Plato was no philistine. It is not the case that Plato
recommended censoring art because he did not understand it or was
unmoved by it; Plato appreciated its power—in fact, he employed
artistic devices to great effect in his own writing; Plato is easily one
of the best writers in the history of philosophy. Nevertheless, he had
real worries about the impact of art, especially upon the young.

In books II and III, the characters discuss children's education,
considering the role of certain art forms (this is unsurprising, given
that the epic poetry of Homer and Hesiod occupied an important
role in ancient Athenian education). The interlocutors express a
concern, for example, that stories depicting the gods as possessing
unethical character traits (as we occasionally find in Homer)
may have a negative effect upon young students. Concerns about
specific subject matter are deepened by the observation that the
young cannot distinguish between direct statement and allegory—
even more troubling is the fact that art's FORMAL characteristics
(e.g., rhythm and musical modes) have the power to make that
which is represented appealing to a young person long before he
can rationally assess its worth. Art appeals to our irrational side,
including the emotions, rather than cultivating our rationality.

The import of these claims is not merely that this sort of education
is inadequate for the perfectly just city but that imitative art can
predispose a young person to become an unjust individual. How
does this work? On Plato's account, there are three parts of the

soul: the rational part (which deliberates), the spirited part (which gets angry and emotional), and the appetitive part (which desires food, drink, sex, money, and so on). In a just soul, the spirited part aligns with the rational part in order to keep the appetites in check. Plato argues that imitative art, as well as certain unfavored rhythms and modes, disrupts the *formation* of this balance in the young, leading the spirited part to align with the appetites, resulting in a malformed, potentially unjust and immoral individual. It is in this light that the following seemingly outlandish claim becomes intelligible: "musical modes are never changed without a change in the most important of a city's laws" (book IV, 424c).

The central criticism that emerges from book X is that artists do not have adequate knowledge of their subject matter. Plato argues that artists are adept at representing a particular subject matter so that it *appears* to be a correct representation but only to those who lack knowledge of that subject matter. Add to this the appealing nature of the *packaging* of the content of a work of art, namely, the formal properties mentioned above, and we have a recipe for socially deleterious art. Those without knowledge of a given topic should not be the ones responsible for educating the young on that topic. When a philosopher possesses knowledge, according to Plato's theory of forms, the object of knowledge is not a material thing but a "form"; by this, he does not mean the structure or shape of a thing; rather, forms are eternal, ideal, immaterial, imperceptible objects knowable only through the intellect.

Consider Plato's example of a bed. Although it is an absurd example, consider what a philosopher knows when she knows what a bed truly is. According to Plato, she does not know this or that physical bed, but the form, a kind of abstract essence of what it is to be a bed, call it *bedness*. When a carpenter makes a bed, she does not *know* the form but she has at least *right opinion*. An artist has neither knowledge nor right opinion of bedness; an artist represents the bed only from a particular perspective. There is a criticism here about the metaphysical status of works of art. Since particular things are imitations of forms, works of art are imitations of these imitations; works of art are images; far removed from real being (the forms).

It is important to note that a portion of Plato's basic critique has had staying power; a portion of the critique is clearly not dependent upon his theory of forms. Critics of the POPULAR ARTS, for example, continue to maintain that artists occasionally present socially dangerous messages that get traction because they are wrapped in enticing packages (art's formal features). After the Columbine school shootings, for instance, a portion of the public discussion that followed involved criticizing the following for negatively influencing the Columbine shooters: the film, *The Matrix* (1999), the heavy metal rock band Judas Priest, and the musician Marilyn Manson. Such criticisms, like Plato's, center on the effects of the arts upon the development of young people. See CENSORSHIP, EMOTION, ETHICS, LITERATURE, TRAGEDY, and MUSIC.

Further Reading

Annas, J. (1981), *An Introduction to Plato's Republic*. Oxford and New York: Oxford University Press.
Naddaff, R. A. (2003), *Exiling the Poets: The Production of Censorship in Plato's Republic*. Chicago and London: University of Chicago Press.
Plato (1992), *The Republic by Plato*, C. D. C. Reeve and G. M. A. Grube (trans.). Indianapolis and Cambridge: Hackett.

The Arts

A number of traditional philosophical theories of art emphasize a property or function that makes something art (see DEFINING ART). For example, works of art possess "significant form" (see FORMALISM, BELL), they afford AESTHETIC EXPERIENCES (DEWEY, BEARDSLEY), they EXPRESS emotions (COLLINGWOOD), or they are REPRESENTATIONAL. Thus, different theories will highlight a certain property or function in each art form. If, for example, a particular philosopher holds that works of art essentially express emotions, then she will aim to explore the way in which visual art expresses emotions, the way in which music expresses emotions, and so on (notice that if the music we consider is *instrumental* music, making sense of how these two arts express emotions is likely to lead us down two very different paths). Consequently, a definition of art will go some way toward directing that theory's approach to particular art forms. Further, insofar as such a theory informs a philosopher's account of artistic VALUE, it will do so regarding each art form as well. However, there is much to say against the viability of such general approaches to DEFINING ART.

The entries in this section are not intended to be comprehensive summaries of what philosophers have said about these art forms (such sections would be much too long, and would not serve the cross-referential flow of this book). Instead, each of these sections serves as an amuse-bouche, as well as serving as a springboard through which readers who want to begin this book *through* an art form can find their way to other entries especially relevant to that art form. These entries are a way of welcoming the reader into debates about ONTOLOGY, INTERPRETATION, DISINTEREST, BEAUTY, POLITICS, and so on, through a discussion of an art form that is of interest to the reader. Most importantly, these entries aim to orient a reader in thinking about a given art form in a philosophical context.

Architecture

Many philosophers of art have emphasized the autonomy of art, whether in terms of the work itself or the experience of it. For example, for the FORMALIST Clive BELL, visual art is essentially *form*, and whatever works of art REPRESENT is irrelevant to their art status and value. For Immanuel KANT, BEAUTY, taste, experiences, and evaluations of works of art are DISINTERESTED; in other words, this traditional view takes it as a mark of the AESTHETIC that practical interests are set aside. Attempting to make sense of architecture in terms of this traditional conception pulls at a basic intuition—how can one be disinterested about a house, airport, or church? Architecture is *designed* to serve practical interests—unlike, for example, sculpture. Buildings that are considered great works of art certainly serve practical purposes; consider cathedrals, government buildings, and concert halls. In fact, architecture seems to be *necessarily* useful. Other arts occasionally perform functions (e.g., a piece of music may serve a religious function) but as regards a work of architecture, successfully performing its function seems crucially important. This does not seem to be the case regarding other arts; we can easily imagine a work of music written for religious worship failing to perform that function while still being considered a great work of music.

One way theorists have traditionally tried to fit architecture into this aesthetic tradition is by suggesting that what makes a useful building an architectural work of art is an aesthetic aspect, where the art status and value rests on that aspect. Buildings become works of art as their appearance is beautified, made aesthetic, through attention to ornamentation, proportion, etc. But if we conceive of the useful aspect of an architectural work of art as too marginal, architecture becomes too similar to sculpture (modern architectural theory, it should be noted, is critical of ornamentation).

Architecture has not always been given a seat at the table; Charles Batteux (1713–80), for example, does not include architecture among the fine arts (see the introduction). Architecture is at the bottom of G. W. F. HEGEL's hierarchy of fine arts; architecture is the most material of the arts, which he takes to be an expressive, representational shortcoming. Hegel maintains that art has the capacity to convey a culture's worldview. In the first phase of art, the symbolic phase, the Egyptian pyramids and temples are examples of architectural works that convey their culture's worldview.

In his "THE ORIGIN OF THE WORK OF ART," Martin HEIDEGGER effectively employs an example of an architectural work to clarify his thought-provoking thesis that works of art open up, or gather together, a "world." For Heidegger, a world is a context that makes meaning possible. A work of art creates the conditions for the possibility of meaning for a culture; as he writes about a Greek temple, "It is the temple work that first structures and simultaneously gathers around itself the unity of those paths and relations in which birth and death, disaster and blessing, victory and disgrace, endurance and decline acquire for the human being shape of its destiny" (2002, pp. 20–1). The Greek temple, in other words, functions as a kind of cultural paradigm.

Architecture is considered in some detail by NELSON GOODMAN. Architectural works of art are distinguished from mere buildings insofar as they function as symbols, as all works of art, on Goodman's view. Relatively few architectural works refer by denoting (the Sydney Opera House, for example, denotes sailboats). More commonly, architectural works refer by *exemplifying*. A symbol that exemplifies refers to one or more of the properties it possesses itself (for simplicity, I am ignoring Goodman's nominalism). Consider a tailor's swatch. While many items of clothing may be made of gabardine, a gabardine swatch is not only made of gabardine (possession), it also refers to gabardine; the swatch is the kind of symbol that exemplifies gabardine. In formalist architecture, works exemplify their structure. Architectural works may also exemplify METAPHORICALLY, which Goodman calls EXPRESSION; for example, a building may metaphorically exemplify movement or freedom. On this view, INTERPRETING a work of architecture is an attempt to understand its reference. While Goodman denies the importance of the architects' *intentions* in determining which interpretation is correct, he is not willing to adopt a relativist position: "A Gothic cathedral that soars and sings does not equally droop and grumble" (1992, p. 646).

Further Reading

Goodman, N. (1992), "How buildings mean," in P. A. Alperson (ed.), *Philosophy of the Visual Arts*. New York: Oxford University Press, pp. 368–76.

Graham, G. (1989), "Art and architecture." *British Journal of Aesthetics*, 29: 248–57.

Heidegger, M. (2002 [1936]), "The origin of the work of art," in J. Young and K. Haynes (eds), *Off the Beaten Track*. Cambridge: Cambridge University Press.

Mitias, M. H. (1994), *Philosophy and Architecture*. Amsterdam: Rodopi.

Scruton, R. (1979), *The Aesthetics of Architecture*. Princeton, NJ: Princeton University Press.

Winters, E. (2007), *Aesthetics and Architecture*. London: Continuum.

Dance

Although dance as a social activity is as old as music, visual art, and the others, dance was not traditionally considered an art in its own right until the eighteenth century. Prior to this time, dance was often considered an element of theatre. Even after the eighteenth century, some philosophers did not include dance among the fine arts. G. W. F. HEGEL, for example, did not include dance within his hierarchy of the fine arts. Due to this history, and due perhaps to the elusive nature of dance itself, it has not garnered philosophy's attention to the degree the other arts have.

The medium of dance is the human body; since body movement is a central dimension of ordinary human activity, philosophers endeavor to distinguish between these ordinary body movements and dance. Traditionally, theorists have attempted to make progress by characterizing dance in terms of philosophical approaches to the other arts. As with the arts in general, in the eighteenth century, influential theories of dance conceived of dance as a REPRESENTATIONAL art; dancers imitate people, situations, emotions, and so on (see the introduction and DEFINING ART). According to such a view, representation is what sets dance apart from ordinary movement. Some of the similarities between dance and music are thought-provoking in critically evaluating this view. Some philosophers have pointed out that a representation-based approach to defining art seems to fail as regards dance insofar as more than a few dance works of art simply do not represent anything (as we find with works of instrumental music); this is especially true if we characterize representation as imitation and consider modern dance.

Consider FORMALISM as a theory of dance. Form is (roughly) the perceptual elements of a work and their relations. In music, these elements are notes related in terms of pitch and time. In dance, form consists of patterns of movements. Just as Eduard Hanslick maintains that music is essentially "tonally moving forms," formalist dance theorists maintain that dance is essentially patterns of movement. As with formalism in general, there is often an accompanying claim that properly apprehending dance forms requires DISINTERESTED perception. According to such a view, what sets dance movement apart from ordinary movement is the special something about the dance movement's form; perhaps the form of a dance work of art is something like what Clive BELL called "significant form."

Given the natural expressiveness of the human body, it is unsurprising that some have favored EXPRESSION theories of dance. On this view, body movement is dance if it expresses emotions. Suzanne Langer (1895–1985) views works of art as symbolic form; works of art are (nondiscursive) symbols. Her approach to expression is not the view Leo Tolstoy espouses, according to which, artists experience an emotion *while* creating, which they then embody in the work (see EMOTION). Rather, artists imagine a feeling, and this *conception* governs their work; such a conception of a feeling is what the dancer presents through an artistic symbol. Although the bodily movement in dance is actual, the gesture of dance is virtual (the gesture is not self-expression; it is a semblance of self-expression). The virtual gestures of dance ultimately symbolize not just any feelings but the feelings of volition, free agency, and so on, which Langer calls "virtual powers." According to expression theory in general, what sets dance movement apart from ordinary movement is that dance movement is expressive in a way that ordinary movement is not; perhaps this special way can be cashed out in terms of *what* is expressed, in terms of the arousal of emotion (as Tolstoy would have it), or in terms of the articulation or clarification of emotion, as R. G. COLLINGWOOD would have it.

But how do we distinguish dance movements from ordinary movements when the dance movements are indistinguishable from ordinary, everyday movements, such as in some postmodern dance. Arthur DANTO's view will be helpful here; he suggests that the features that distinguish a work of art from something that is not a work of art are nonexhibited; works of art are *about* something; they possess meaning that requires interpretation, which must take into account the work's art-historical context.

ONTOLOGY is another area of the philosophy of dance that resembles the philosophy of music. It is common to draw a distinction between dance works and dance performances; a distinction often drawn regarding music. Perhaps a given work of dance is a *type*, a pattern, or sequence of movements; a performance of the work by a particular dance company on a particular occasion is a *token* of that type (in which that sequence of movements is carried out). Musical works are often conceived as abstract types, and performances as tokens. What makes one performance or another a performance of a given dance work? Again, this problem of identity arises in music as well. Philosophers such as Nelson GOODMAN have attempted to answer this question by appealing to dance notation, as they often do in relation to music; performances that comply with a work's notation are identified as performances of that work (for Goodman, full compliance is required). However, the relative imprecision of dance notation, and the lack of a standard notation, makes this an especially problematic maneuver.

Further Reading

Beardsley, M. (1982), "What is going on in a dance?" *Dance Research Journal*, 15: 31–7.
Langer, S. K. (1953), *Feeling and Form: A Theory of Art Developed from Philosophy in A New Key*. New York: Scribner.
McFee, G. (1992), *Understanding Dance*. London: Routledge.
Sheets-Johnstone, M. (ed.) (1984), *Illuminating Dance*. Lewisberg: Bucknell. University Press.
Sparshott, F. (1988), *Off the Ground: First Steps to a Philosophical Consideration of the Dance*. Princeton, NJ: Princeton University Press.

Film

Very early in the history of filmmaking, philosophical questions, which will be familiar to readers of this book, were asked by film theorists. Is film art? What is unique about this artistic medium among the arts? (See the INTRODUCTION and DEFINING ART.) Increasingly, philosophers have been contributing to these debates. The psychologist Rudolph Arnheim (1904–2007) holds that film is a unique medium in its focus on the moving visual image. But in order for film to achieve art status, it cannot merely reproduce reality (see REPRESENTATION); he emphasizes that features such as editing enable film to do more than simply record reality; such features supply the means for shaping subject matter and thus allow for artistic expression (Arnheim maintains that works of art necessarily involve the EXPRESSION of emotions). Adding sound to film is a corruption of its specific medium (the moving image). Sound films are also more realistic, less abstract, than silent films. In light of such differences, Arnheim maintains that silent film surpasses sound film in artistic merit.

The contrary, realist view is held by the critic André Bazin (1918–58). Bazin emphasizes the photographic core of the medium of film, and claims that film ought to pursue its unique ability to record reality. The essence of film is mechanical production. (Noël Carroll rejects the notion that film consists of a specific medium with essential features.) The notion that film reveals its subject matter in a more direct way than, say, painting, is elucidated by Kendall WALTON. In paintings, we do not directly see the objects depicted; the painters' beliefs affect the rendering of the depicted objects. Film is a mechanical medium in that this mediation is absent; the relation between a subject and their representation on film is causal.

Philosophers concerned with the ONTOLOGY of works of art wonder about the kind of thing a work of art is, what kind of entity. Are works of art physical things, mental entities, abstract objects? An important distinction among these considerations is that some art forms involve singular works of art (paintings, frescoes, polaroids) and others, multiple (music, literature, and film). While the *Mona Lisa* exists only in one place at one time, *Citizen Kane* has had innumerable screenings. Related to this ontological distinction, Walter BENJAMIN considered the way in which film, photography, and recorded music center on technical reproducibility. He argued that the experience of these mass arts differs from traditional experiences of painting, (noncast) sculpture, and so on. Traditionally, due to their singularity and uniqueness, we experienced paintings as possessing an "aura," as mysterious, distant, and unapproachable. But the technical reproducibility of film, and other mass arts, removes this aura. Benjamin, a MARXIST, takes this new art and experience to have POLITICALLY progressive implications. As art moves away from the ritualistic model, spectators are released from their reverential engagement; they are permitted a critical distance. In addition, POPULAR ART opens one up to engaging communally; seeing a film at a movie theater is a communal experience. Contrast this with Theodor W. ADORNO'S negative view of the effect popular art has on politics.

Other issues philosophers have begun to examine since the 1990s include a consideration of the identity of the film artist. Regarding painting or poetry, it is straightforward (at least initially) to formulate an expression theory of art: an artist expresses her EMOTION through her art—but what about film? One traditional answer is that the film artist or author is the director, the auteur. But what should we say about large-scale film productions that involve a number of creative influences (screenwriter, actors, cinematographer, set director, and so on)? See PHOTOGRAPHY.

Further Reading

Arnheim, R. (1957), *Film as Art*. Berkeley: University of California Press.
Bazin, A. (1967), *What is Cinema? Volume I*. Hugh Gray (trans.).
    Berkeley: University of California Press.
Bogue, R. (2003), *Deleuze on Cinema*. New York and London: Routledge.
Carroll, N. (1988), *Philosophical Problems of Classical Film Theory*.
    Princeton, NJ: Princeton University Press.
Walton, K. (1984), "Transparent pictures: On the nature of photographic realism." *Critical Inquiry*, 11: 246–77.

Literature

For about 200 years, "literature" has referred to texts written with imagination; here, we will focus on poetry, prose fiction, and drama. How does literature fare regarding the standard approaches to DEFINING ART in general? PLATO, ARISTOTLE, and philosophers for many centuries, understood dramatic poetry (Greek tragedy) to be a kind of imitation, REPRESENTATION. In Greek tragedy, the actors imitate events. The imitation view is less viable regarding literature of other kinds. A FORMALIST view of literature de-emphasizes subject matter while emphasizing literary devices (form) such as rhyme, meter, and plot structure. The key literary device for the Russian Formalists is the defamiliarization of words, which can lead a reader to adopt a fresh perspective on various issues. On a formalist view, literary devices are definitive of the literary work of art. Literature may present the most difficult challenge to a strict formalism that takes representational content to be entirely irrelevant. Is it possible to hold a view that understands what novels are *about* to be irrelevant to a novel's art status? See BELL, *ART*.

In his *Laocoön* (1766), Gotthold Ephraim Lessing (1729–81) adopts the imitation theory but emphasizes that each art form employs a different means of imitation. Poetry consists of words arranged consecutively; painting consists of elements "arranged side by side," simultaneously presented. Lessing maintains that this implies that different art forms are primarily suited to represent different subject matter: poetry is primarily suited to represent actions; painting, objects.

Some philosophers have attempted to define art in general in terms of the expression of EMOTIONS. Literature may express the emotions of the artist, arouse emotions in readers, as well as express the emotions of a narrator or characters (one thing that makes fiction interesting is that a reader often gets access to a character's emotions from the inside, so to speak). On this view, what makes literature art are the emotions expressed. Another standard approach to defining art centers on AESTHETIC EXPERIENCE; a novel, for example, can more or less control a reader's attention, guiding her through a series of events in order to afford a particular aesthetic experience (see DEWEY, *ART AS EXPERIENCE*).

Philosophers have long considered the differences between literature and philosophy. While, according to a broad definition of literature, philosophy just is literature, if literature is understood as involving poetic language and artistic devices, some philosophers have emphasized the differences. In fact, there is an ancient rift between philosophy and poetry. Plato stresses that philosophers can possess and convey knowledge, poets cannot. According to Plato, poetry is dangerous to society; he bans poetry from his ideal state (see PLATO, *THE REPUBLIC*, CENSORSHIP). Aristotle disagrees, taking the view that, through its depiction of specific characters and their actions, poetry can convey general truths about human affairs. Plato also claims that poetry arouses the emotions, endangering reason's governance of the self. Aristotle again disagrees, holding that tragedy has a therapeutic effect on spectators; the spectators undergo a kind of catharsis, which, according to one interpretation, is a purging. Emotions such as fear and pity can be aroused in the spectators of a tragedy, and this experience vents these emotions, which otherwise may be disruptive. (See ETHICS; ARISTOTLE, *THE POETICS*).

A number of philosophers have rated literature as the highest of the art forms, in one sense or another. G. W. F. Hegel, for example, believes that poetry is best able to convey the ethos of the modern, Christian age. Poetry can embody more complexities than other art forms by engaging the imagination, by being less dependent upon the physical, and by being more intimate (see HEGEL, *LECTURES ON FINE ART*). NIETZSCHE offers a theory of tragedy in terms of underlying psychological drives that he associates with Greek deities. The Apollonian is characterized by clarity, appearance, dream, self-control, and beauty. The Dionysian is characterized by intoxication, loss of self, and the SUBLIME. Most arts grow out of predominantly one drive or the other; Greek tragedy involves both.

There is a puzzle about the emotions and fiction. Readers often react emotionally to characters and situations in fiction; for example, we might feel pity, fear, or feel happy for a character due to her circumstances in a story. In order to feel pity for someone, it seems we need to believe that the person is actually in a pitiable situation (this paradox assumes a cognitivist view of the emotions). But of course, a character in fiction, and her situation, is fictional. This is known as "the paradox of fiction." Kendall WALTON's influential solution to this paradox is that the beliefs involved are fictional, and the fear, and so on, that we experience in these situations is only quasifear. Others maintain that we do experience real emotions in relation to fiction, and instead deny that believing in the reality of the characters and situations is required for experiencing such emotions.

Literature raises interesting ONTOLOGICAL questions. What kind of thing is a literary work of art? It does not seem right to hold that the work is a physical thing. We might maintain that a literary work is the original manuscript. But this seems wrong. If that manuscript were destroyed in a fire, we would not conclude that the work ceased to exist. R. G. Collingwood puts forward an idealist ontology. He holds that a poem, for example, may exist even though it has never been written or spoken. It exists in the artist's head. The literary work of art is a mental object (see COLLINGWOOD, *THE PRINCIPLES OF ART*). Roman Ingarden presents an ontology of the literary work that involves both physical and ideal aspects; the work is an intentional object, a "stratified formation" (see PHENOMENOLOGY). A literary work is different from a painting in that a given painting exists only in one place; there are numerous copies of *Anna Karenina*. What makes a copy of Anna Karenina a copy of that literary work?

A number of issues already raised surface again when we consider approaches to the INTERPRETATION of literary works. If a literary work is like a conversation, then interpreting ought to involve prioritizing the author's intentions. This traditional view is on display in expression theories such as Tolstoy's (see EMOTION). The Russian Formalists, structuralists, and those affiliated with the movement of New Criticism maintain that the interpretive emphasis should be placed on the work itself; the author's intentions are irrelevant. The locus classicus of this position is W. K. Wimsatt and Monroe BEARDSLEY'S "The Intentional Fallacy," in which they argue that if an author's intended meaning is *not* successfully realized in a literary work, then her intentions are not instructive in uncovering the meaning or evaluating the work; if her intended meaning *is* realized in the work, then we can disregard those intentions and simply focus on the work. Importantly, on this set of views, there is still one, correct interpretation of a text, which is fixed by the work itself, linguistic structures.

Poststructuralists, such as Roland BARTHES, Michel Foucault (1926–84), and Jacques Derrida (1930–2004) go further. They argue that there is not one, correct interpretation or understanding of a text. It was easy to grasp how one might think that an author can be the source of a text's fixed meaning, but once the author is eliminated, what foundation remains? These philosophers argue that the work's structure is open to multiple interpretations. They see this as the liberation of the reader. See METAPHOR; SCHOPENHAUER.

Further Reading

Currie, G. (1990), *The Nature of Fiction*. Cambridge: Cambridge University Press.

Davies, D. and Matheson, C. (2008), *Contemporary Readings in the Philosophy of Literature: An Analytic Approach*. Peterborough, Ontario: Broadview Press.

John, E. and Lopes, D. M. (eds) (2004), *The Philosophy of Literature: Contemporary and Classic Readings—An Anthology*. Oxford: Wiley-Blackwell.

Lamarque, P. V. and Olsen, S. H. (1994), *Truth, Fiction, and Literature: A Philosophical Perspective*. Oxford: Clarendon Press.

Music

PLATO was famously worried about the effects of music; music can stir the emotions to an extent that may hamper a person's rationality. If maudlin emotions are stirred, a person's character can be negatively affected. He was especially worried about these issues regarding the young. This was no marginal issue for Plato; he defines justice as a certain balance among the parts of an individual, and this balance can be thrown off by the wrong music; he goes so far as to claim that the "musical modes are never changed without a change in the most important of a city's laws" (book IV, 424c). (See PLATO, *REPUBLIC*.)

The relationship between music and the EMOTIONS has never ceased to be a central concern in the philosophy of music. Some theorists reject the importance of the connection. For example, Eduard Hanslick (1825–1904) was adamant that if we want to understand the nature of instrumental music, we should *not* focus on the emotions aroused or REPRESENTED in the music; regarding the former, attempting to understand the aesthetic principles of music through emotional reactions is, he thought, akin to attempting to understand the nature of wine by getting drunk. After all, isn't an emotional reaction to music idiosyncratic? Hanslick, a FORMALIST, argued that the focus should be on musical structure, form. According to Hanslick, the content of music is "tonally moving forms."

Some have maintained that music is the art with the most intimate connection to the emotions. Perhaps music's arousal of the emotions is instructive, or perhaps the crucial relation is music's EXPRESSION of emotions. It is puzzling to understand just how music can express emotion. This question is even more challenging in light of philosophers' traditional assumption that we should only be considering instrumental music (the idea being that we ought to focus on music itself, not music and lyrics, for example, where the lyrics may do the lion's share of expressive work). A novel can express emotion through a character's words, actions, and on—how can instrumental music accomplish this? Consider the view of Peter Kivy. Rather than sad music being an expression of a composer's sadness, sad music is *expressive of* sadness. Drawing upon an analogy to sad-looking Saint Bernards, Kivy points out that Saint Bernards look sad even when they are happy; the sadness we perceive is not an *expression* of a Saint Bernard's sadness; rather, Saint Benards' faces have particular, droopy features that make them *look* sad. Similarly, sad music has particular contours—features of the music's form, such as a slow tempo and halting rhythm—in virtue of which, it *sounds* sad. This sadness is a property of the music itself; it is an emergent, perceptual property of the music, in the same way that cheerfulness is a property of the color yellow.

Suzanne Langer (1895–1985) agrees that there is a deep connection between the feelings and music, but she does not believe that arousal or expression theories capture this connection. Music, according to Langer, is a special kind of symbol, a nondiscursive symbol (language consists of discursive symbols). She maintains that music presents the forms of feelings; music is *about* feelings. Music accomplishes this by means of its formal structure; the forms of feeling are isomorphic with the forms of music.

What kind of thing is a musical work? A musical work does not seem to be identical to its score, not even an original copy of its score; a work does not seem to be identical to a performance, not even a set of performances (see ONTOLOGY). An influential view of musical works maintains that works are *types*, sound-structures. The pure, Platonist version of this view maintains that works are timeless, eternal sound-structures. One shortcoming of this view is that it results in the counterintuitive position that musical works are not created but discovered. Jerrold Levinson holds that musical works are *created* abstract objects, contextualized types. According to Levinson, musical works are not merely sound structures; they also involve relational properties concerning the composer, the work's musico-historical context (these properties are what make claims of originality possible), and instrumentation specifications. Lydia Goehr argues that in order to correctly determine which preontological and aesthetic issues are relevant to musical ontology, an historical examination of musical practice is required. Goehr carries out a genealogy, tracing the emergence of the concept of the musical work in the practice, articulating its elements and the implications for musical ontology. Until fairly recently, philosophers have focused upon classical music. It may be that other genres of music are ontologically different. Theodore Gracyk has claimed that the musical work in rock is neither a structure nor a performance; rather, the musical work is the recording.

What is musical experience? When we hear music, we do not merely hear sounds, according to Roger Scruton, we hear *tones*. We hear mere sounds as conveying information (e.g., the sound of screeching tires indicates an abruptly stopping car); we hear musical tones as ends in themselves; when the sounds of musical instruments become experientially detached from their sources, and are heard as organized in terms of pitch, rhythm, melody, and harmony, they become tones. This is what Scruton calls "the acousmatic experience of sound." Note that the experiential detaching involved here resembles the more common DISINTEREST of AESTHETIC EXPERIENCE. For a criticism of such disinterest see BOURDIEU. Also see POPULAR ART, POLITICS, ADORNO, and SCHOPENHAUER.

Further Reading

Budd, M. (1985), *Music and the Emotions*. London: Routledge.

Davies, S. (2001), *Musical Works and Performances*. Oxford: Clarendon Press.

Goehr, L. (1994), *The Imaginary Museum of Musical Works*. Oxford: Clarendon Press.

Gracyk, T. (1996), *Rhythm and Noise: An Aesthetics of Rock*. Durham: Duke University Press.

Gracyk, T. and Kania, A. (2011), *The Routledge Companion to Philosophy and Music*. London and New York: Routledge.

Kivy, P. (1989), *Sound Sentiment*. Philadelphia: Temple University Press.

Levinson, J. (1980), "What a musical work is." *Journal of Philosophy*, 77: 5–28.

Scruton, R. (1997), *The Aesthetics of Music*. Oxford: Oxford University Press.

Photography

Unlike other pictorial REPRESENTATIONS (paintings and drawings), there seems to be something more real, direct, and immediate about this medium. This was not lost on painters during the period of photography's emergence. In the words of the French film theorist and critic André Bazin (1918–58), photography "freed Western painting, once and for all, from its obsession with realism and allowed it to recover its aesthetic autonomy" (1960, p. 9). Photography's directness is a function of the mechanical nature of the process of photography. A number of thinkers, Bazin included, have agreed that when we look at a photograph of (say) Joan Crawford, we see Joan herself.

Similarly, Kendall WALTON claims that photographs are transparent in the sense that we see what is pictured through the photograph, somewhat like we see a person through a window or objects through a telescope. In paintings, we do not directly see the objects depicted; we do not see *through* paintings to their subjects; painters' beliefs affect the rendering of the depicted objects. In photography, this mediation of an artist is absent. The relation between a photograph's subject matter and a photographic image is causal, occurring by means of light.

It is not surprising that photography's mechanical nature, and the seemingly limited scope of the photographer's involvement (as compared to artists working in other art forms), has led theorists to consider it to be an automated medium of recording, and thus to question its status as an art (see DEFINING ART). The general idea is that in order for an artist to EXPRESS herself, convey meaning, or construct a work that is valuable in terms of its FORM or ability to afford AESTHETIC EXPERIENCES, she needs a medium that can be shaped, a medium that can be *worked*. Consider the centrality of the artist's manipulation of the materials for an expression theory of art. According to Leo Tolstoy (see EMOTION), an artist begins with her experience of an emotion. She then places lines on a canvas (say) for the purpose of infecting viewers with that same emotion. Paintings that result in arousing in a spectator the same emotion the artist experienced are works of art.

Although he limits himself to an ideal, pure notion of photography, Roger Scruton claims that the intentions of photographers are not central to the medium; photography is not even properly a representational art. Whatever emotional or AESTHETIC PROPERTIES a photograph possesses, they are properties of the photograph's subject, not the photograph itself. One way to defend photography from this sort of critique is to point out the innumerable ways in which photographers do insert themselves into the process, interpreting their subject matter by shaping their product. For example, photographers *compose* their photographs; they frame their subject matter in one way or another. Photographers choose camera angles. In controlled conditions, they choose lighting. In postproduction, they make any number of choices about contrast, tone, brightness, color, and so on. (Scruton has an answer to such a reply: through this kind of activity, the work becomes less like pure photography and more like painting.)

In contrast to the very limited ways in which traditional works of art can be reproduced, Walter BENJAMIN explores the fact that photographic images can be reproduced in great numbers, mechanically (like films and recorded music). As a result, photographs do not have the "aura" of traditional arts such as painting and sculpture. This aura is a quality of our experience of these traditional objects; we experience these objects as possessing a reverential, mysterious dimension; they are distant and unapproachable; this is due to their singularity, uniqueness, and authenticity. Benjamin emphasizes the positive ramifications of the evaporation of aura. Technological reproduction enables works of art to engage viewers within the viewers' own environments, no longer in museums and concert halls alone. This is an emancipation for art and spectators; art is freed from tradition and location. This allows for new ways of experiencing works of art, and new POLITICAL forms of art. Traditional ways of engaging with art emphasize ideas such as eternal value, mystery, genius, and ritual; Benjamin, a MARXIST, sees this tradition as associated with capitalism, and as paving the way for fascism. Mass art (see POPULAR ART), in contrast, possesses a liberating, politically critical, and progressive potential. As art moves away from the ritualistic model, spectators are released from their reverential engagement; they are permitted a critical distance. Furthermore, popular art opens us up to engaging communally; seeing a film at a movie theater, for example, is a communal experience.

In his *Camera Lucida* (1980), Roland BARTHES proposes a thought-provoking manner of conceiving of the content of photographs, drawing a distinction between two themes or aspects of photographs: the *studium* and the *punctum*. The *studium* consists of a photograph's culturally coded, symbolic meanings, which are available to an average viewer; this is its manifest, obvious meaning. The *punctum* cosists of a feature (or features) of a photograph that punctuate the *studium*, a detail in the photograph that disrupts the obvious meaning of a photograph, and which has a decisive effect upon the viewer. Regarding the *punctum*, Barthes writes, "it is this element which rises from the scene, shoots out of it like an arrow, and pierces me" (1980, p. 26). A part of what makes the *punctum* so effective is that it is an element of a photograph that does not fit; it is not intelligible from within the standard symbolism, and in some sense, it eludes understanding. Later, in *Camera Lucida*, Barthes articulates another *punctum*; it is not a mere detail in a photograph but concerns the way in which photographs present objects to us both as present, and at the same time, as being in the past ("that-has-been"). See FILM.

Further Reading

Barthes, R. (1980), *Camera Lucida*, R. Howard (trans.). New York: Hill and Wang.
Bazin, A. (1960 [1945]), "The Ontology of the Photographic Image." H. Gray (trans.), *Film Quarterly*, 13: 4–9.
Maynard, P. (1997), *The Engine of Visualization: Thinking through Photography*. Ithaca, NY: Cornell University Press.
Scruton, R. (ed.) (1983). "Photography and Representation," in *The Aesthetic Understanding: Essays in The Philosophy of Art and Culture*. London: Methuen, pp. 102–26.
Sontag, S. (1979), *On Photography*. Harmondsworth: Penguin.

Tragedy

In PLATO'S *REPUBLIC* we find a deep concern about the power of the arts to stir the emotions. Plato worries less about *why* spectators seek to have their EMOTIONS stirred and more about the dangers to society of a populace directed by their emotions rather than reason. What is more, unlike philosophers, tragic poets do not truly understand their subject matter; thus, such works of art convey falsehoods. Tragedy stirs the "negative" emotions: fear, pity, anxiety, sorrow, and so on. What good can come from stirring these emotions and REPRESENTING falsehoods? The danger runs deep: Plato believes that a just individual possesses a soul in which reason, the emotions, and the appetites are balanced. This balance can be derailed, or never established, as a result of the influence of arts such as tragedy.

In his POETICS, ARISTOTLE looked upon the effects of tragedy in a much more positive light. He claims that the experience of tragedy purges or vents the negative emotions, which, unpurged, may be psychologically disruptive. In fact, this CATHARSIS is the purpose of tragedy, according to Aristotle. An alternate interpretation of Aristotle's point construes catharsis as a kind of clarification of emotions; through the experience of a tragedy, a spectator *calibrates* her emotions; she learns when it is appropriate to experience an emotion such as pity, to what degree, and so on. Either way, tragedy contributes to our psychological well-being. In addition, and in further contrast with Plato, Aristotle maintains that we can learn from tragedies; through its depiction of specific characters and their actions tragedy can convey general truths about human affairs.

For eighteenth-century philosophers, the "paradox of tragedy" referred to the odd fact that we find experiences of tragedy *pleasing* even though "negative" emotions, such as sorrow and anxiety, lie at the center of these experiences. In his "On Tragedy" (1757), DAVID HUME argues that when a tragedy is well made, the pleasure we experience as a result of its quality overwhelms and "converts" the negative emotions. Hume's view involves the clarification that the negative emotions result from the subject matter, whereas the pleasure results from the quality of the tragedy's construction.

NIETZSCHE'S account of tragedy, found in his *The Birth of Tragedy*, rests on two central notions, the Dionysian and the Apollonian, which are forces or drives that he names after the Greek deities. He uses these terms in discussing metaphysics, psychology, and art. The Apollonian is characterized by clarity, appearance, dream, self-control, and BEAUTY. The Dionysian is characterized by intoxication, loss of self, and the SUBLIME (i.e., awe-inspiring and overpowering). Some art forms are predominantly Apollonian, such as sculpture, painting, and epic poetry; other art forms are predominantly Dionysian, such as music and dance. Still others are a more balanced combination of the two forces, such as Greek tragedy. In Nietzsche's early work, he adopted SCHOPENHAUER'S bleak view of human existence. Through the creation of art, these drives sublimate the despair of the human condition. Greek tragedy has its origins in the chorus component, which showed the Greek spectators the bleak truth about human life (the chorus is the Dionysian aspect of tragedy), while simultaneously making that truth bearable through the detached, aesthetic representation (this occurs insofar as the characters are present as if in a dream, an illusion; this is the Apollonian aspect). Retaining the Dionysian element is important; tragedy does not avoid facing the truths of human existence, as do more purely Apollonian arts, such as epic poetry. See LITERATURE.

Further Reading

Hume, D. (1993), "Of tragedy," in S. Copley and A. Edgar (eds), *Hume: Selected Essays.* Oxford: Oxford University Press.
Nietzsche, F. (1999 [1872]), *The Birth of Tragedy and Other Writings*, R. Geuss and R. Speirs (eds), R. Speirs (trans.). Cambridge: Cambridge University Press.

Visual Art

The visual arts are commonly thought to include painting, drawing, sculpture, FILM, PHOTOGRAPHY, and sometimes ARCHITECTURE (taking architecture to be a visual art is to underplay its functional dimension). The oldest and most common way of DEFINING ART in general, REPRESENTATION as imitation, seems to fit nicely with the visual arts. The idea is that works of art represent their subject matter by resembling it. A painting represents a landscape by copying it; a sculpture of a person imitates the person's features, posture, and expression. On this view, what makes an artifact a work of art is imitation. By the eighteenth century, BEAUTY had been attached to imitation (see the introduction). In his *Laocoön* (1766), Gotthold Ephraim Lessing (1729–81) adopts the imitation theory but emphasizes that each art form employs a different means of imitation. Painting consists of elements "arranged side by side," simultaneously presented; poetry consists of words arranged consecutively. Lessing maintains that this implies that different art forms are primarily suited to represent different subject matter: painting is primarily suited to represent objects; poetry, actions.

Regarding visual arts that involve pictorial representation (painting, drawing, and so on), twentieth-century philosophers have been critical of the view that takes pictorial representation to be a matter of resemblance. Philosophers have considered the extent to which pictures represent through symbolization (see Nelson GOODMAN) or special kinds of visual experiences; for example, Richard WOLLHEIM claims that pictorial representation consists of a special kind of twofold perceptual experience in which we see represented objects *in* a painting at the same time that we perceive a painting's surface features (brush strokes, and so on).

Although Clive BELL'S FORMALISM is often entertained as a definition of art in general (see DEFINING ART), it is presented by Bell as a theory of visual art. In his *ART*, Bell focuses attention toward the structural designs of visual art; he claims that the defining feature of visual art is a special kind of form, what he calls "significant form." A viewer knows which artifacts possess significant form, because, when these are perceived, they arouse in us "the aesthetic emotion." Bell's view is particularly adept at dealing with visual art that downplays subject matter, such as abstract art. In fact, Bell claims that what a work of art is about, its representational content, is irrelevant to its status as a work of art.

What kind of thing is a visual work of art? This is the question of ONTOLOGY. It seems reasonable to maintain that visual works of art are physical things, unlike the more problematic cases of literature, music, dance, and so on. Critics of a physical ontology will point out that a painted canvas has properties that a painting, the work of art, does not have; for example, *this* painted canvas weighs three pounds. Furthermore, the work of art has properties that the painted canvas lacks; for example, the work of art has representational properties that the canvas lacks. Such considerations lead John DEWEY to argue that art *is* experience (in the specific sense he articulates). Paintings seem to be clear counter-examples to idealist ontologies, such as R. G. COLLINGWOOD'S, which conceives of all works of art as mental entities; this may seem *somewhat* reasonable regarding music but an important aspect of painting is its material embodiment, paint on canvas (see PHENOMENOLOGY).

Sculpture, often ignored by philosophers, occupies a special place in G. W. F. Hegel's philosophy of art. For Hegel, art's aim is to convey the ethos of a culture, but this is also the aim of philosophy and religion. In Hegel's account of history, either art, religion, or philosophy best convey a particular epoch's ethos. In the classical Greek period, art expresses the Greek ethos better than philosophy or religion, and sculpture does this better than the other art forms.

Greek sculpture represents the free individuality of the Greek gods, which is an expression of the Greeks' ethos. This embodiment of the freedom of spirit is what Hegel calls "true" or "ideal" beauty. See HEGEL, *LECTURES ON FINE ART*. Arthur DANTO'S definition of art, as well as George DICKIE'S institutional theory of art, maintains that the definitive features of works of art—including visual works of art—are imperceptible, nonexhibited. According to Danto, the nonexhibited features include a work of art's possessing meaning and requiring interpretation. Danto's theory has proven to be useful for making sense of avant-garde art, including installations. See PHOTOGRAPHY, FILM.

Further Reading

Alperson, P. A. (ed.) (1992), *The Philosophy of the Visual Arts*. Oxford: Oxford University Press.

Barthes, R. (2010), *Camera Lucida: Reflections on Photography*, R. Howard (trans.). New York: Hill and Wang.

Gombrich, E. H. (1960), *Art and Illusion: A Study in the Psychology of Pictorial Representation* (2nd revised edn). New York and Princeton: Princeton University Press.

Lessing, G. (1957 [1766]), *Laocoön: An Essay upon the Limits of Painting and Poetry*, E. Frothingham (trans.). New York: Noonday Press.

A Guide to Further Reading

Introductory Texts

Beardsley, M. (1966), *Aesthetics from Classical Greece to the Present.* University of Alabama Press.

Carroll, N. (1999), *Philosophy of Art: A Contemporary Introduction.* Routledge Press.

Davies, S. (2006), *The Philosophy of Art.* Wiley-Blackwell.

Eaton, M. (1999), *Basic Issues in Aesthetics.* Waveland.

Eldridge, R. (2003), *An Introduction to the Philosophy of Art.* Cambridge University Press.

Fisher, J. A. (1992), *Reflecting on Art.* Mayfield.

Gracyk, T. (2011), *The Philosophy of Art: An Introduction.* Polity.

Graham, G. (2005), *Philosophy of the Arts: An Introduction to Aesthetics.* Routledge Press.

Lyas, C. (1997). *Aesthetics.* London: UCL Press.

Stecker, R. (2012), *Aesthetics and the Philosophy of Art: An Introduction.* Rowman & Littlefield.

Handbooks, Companions, etc.

Alperson, P. A. (ed.) (1992), *The Philosophy of the Visual Arts.* Oxford: Oxford University Press.

Davies, S., Higgins, K. M., Hopkins, R., Stecker R., and Cooper, D. E. (eds) (2009), *A Companion to Aesthetics.* Wiley-Blackwell.

Giovannelli, A. (ed.) (2012), *Aesthetics: The Key Thinkers.* Continuum.

Gracyk, T. and Kania, A. (eds) (2011), *The Routledge Companion to Philosophy and Music.* Routledge Press.

Kivy, P. (ed.) (2004), *The Blackwell Guide to Aesthetics.* Wiley-Blackwell.

Levinson, J. (ed.) (2005), *The Oxford Handbook of Aesthetics.* Oxford University Press.

Lopes, D. M. and Gaut, B. (eds) (2005), *The Routledge Companion to Aesthetics*. Routledge Press.
Ribeiro, A. C. (ed.) (2012), *The Continuum Companion to Aesthetics*. Continuum.

Anthologies

Adams, H. (ed.) (1981), *Critical Theory Since Plato*. Harcourt Brace Jovanovich, Inc.
Dickie, G., Sclafani, R., and Roblin R. (eds) (1989), *Aesthetics: A Critical Anthology*. New York: St Martin's Press.
Feagin, S. (ed.) (1998), *Aesthetics*. Oxford University Press.
Goldblatt, D. and Brown, L. B. (eds) (2005), *A Reader in Philosophy of the Arts*. Pearson Prentice Hall.
Hofstadter, A. and Kuhns, R. (eds) (1976), *Philosophies of Art and Beauty: Selected Readings in Aesthetics from Plato to Heidegger*. University Of Chicago Press.
Janaway, C. (ed.) (2005), *Reading Aesthetics and Philosophy of Art: Selected Texts with Interactive Commentary*. Wiley-Blackwell.
Kearney, R. and Rasmussen, D. (eds) (2001), *Continental Aesthetics: Romanticism to Postmodernism: An Anthology*. Wiley-Blackwell.
Kennick, W. E. (ed.) (1979), *Art and Philosophy: Readings in Aesthetics*. New York: St Martin's Press.
Lamarque, P. and Olsen, S. H. (eds) (2003), *Aesthetics and the Philosophy of Art: The Analytic Tradition: An Anthology*. Wiley-Blackwell.
Neill, A. and Ridley, A. (eds) (1995), *The Philosophy of Art: Readings Ancient and Modern*. New York: McGraw-Hill.
Ross, S. (ed.) (1994), *Art and Its Significance: An Anthology of Aesthetic Theory*. State University of New York Press.
Tanke, J. J. and McQuillan, C. (eds) (2012), *The Bloomsbury Anthology of Aesthetics*. Continuum.
Weitz, M. (1959), *Problems in Aesthetics*. The Macmillan Company.

Encyclopedias

Borchert, D. M. (ed.) (2006), *Encyclopedia of Philosophy* (Second Edition; ten volumes). Macmillan Reference; Thomson Gale. (Although a general encyclopedia of philosophy, this work contains many well-written entries in the philosophy of art).

Craig, E. (ed.) (1998), *Routledge Encyclopedia of Philosophy* (ten volumes). London and New York: Routledge Press. (Although a general encyclopedia of philosophy, this work contains many well-written entries in the philosophy of art).

Kelly, M. (ed.) (1998), *Encyclopedia of Aesthetics* (four volumes). New York and Oxford: Oxford University Press.

Zalta, Edward N. (ed.), *The Stanford Encyclopedia of Philosophy*. http:// plato.stanford.edu/ (Although a general encyclopedia of philosophy, this work contains many well-written entries in the philosophy of art).

INDEX